2000

May the Lord of
power and love use
this book to reveal His
infinite understanding. Psalm 147:5

Because He came,

Jean

Gaze at God
Glance at All Else

fran miller

Gaze at God, Glance at All Else
ISBN 0-9665424-4-4
Second Printing

Copyright © 1999 by Fran D Miller
Edited by K Nicole Rowland
Published by The Master Design
  PO Box 17865
  Memphis, TN 38187-0865
  info@masterdesign.org
  www.masterdesign.org

Photo of Fran Miller by Olan Mills.

Printed in the United States of America
by Evangel Press, Nappanee, IN 46550

I dedicate this book to
my three children,
Lori, Allison, and Justin.

You taught me
what real love
looks like and acts like.

Contents

Acknowledgements

First and foremost, I want to thank the One who owns the world, and yet chose to go to the cross for me. To the Lord Jesus, I owe my life, and I thank Him for calling me and enabling me to write this book.

Special thanks go to my editor, Nicole Rowland, who was an answer to prayer. One week after I asked the LORD to send me an editor that could put the necessary band-aids and braces on this book, Nicole sat across the table from me and shared that one of her heart's desires was to be an editor. I knew God had brought her into my life to help with this book. I thank her for all the countless hours she spent with me and offered suggestions that I wish I had thought of myself. I thank Nicole for believing in this book and encouraging me all along the way.

I thank my publisher, Faithe Finley, who not only designed the cover, formatted and polished this book, but who has become a special friend. How many publishers do you know that would bring you chocolate ice cream late at night because she heard you were weary and discouraged? And how many publishers do you know that would bring you medicine when you were sick? I thank Faithe for always going the extra mile.

I thank Bible Study Fellowship, the instrument God chose to use in my life to teach me how to study, understand and apply His Word to my own life. Without this beginning, there would not be a book.

To my spiritual mentors and teaching leaders, MaryAnn Frazier and Jonetta Fargarson, I owe my sincere thanks for their example and teachings that inspired me to depend on Jesus and to desire to look more like Him. Their love gave me the confidence to share Jesus with you in this book.

To the class I taught for 13 years, I thank you for your prayers and for the gift of my laptop computer that made the writing of this book much easier.

I thank my sister, Lynda, for sharing her gift of encouragement with me. After writing the first page of this book at her house 5 years ago, I put it away for a couple of years. Believing God had called me to write this book, she never stopped encouraging me to finish what God had started. Thank you, Lynda, for following 1 Thessalonians 5:11: "Therefore encourage one another, and build up one another." I love you dearly.

I thank all my dear friends who have prayed and pushed me to complete this assignment. Your prayers went to the very throne room of God and were honored. Every one of you is a part of each page.

I also wish to thank my sister-in-law, Debbie Dlugach, for making this book possible. Her love and support and encouragement gave me assurance this book should be published.

I also thank my two added gifts from God. My sons-in-law, David and Dan, for loving my girls and helping them understand all the times I couldn't be with them during the writing of this book.

I thank my brother Phillip for surprising me by having the ribbons put in each book. I love that he is a part of every book that is read. He must be crazy about me! Anyone who knows me well, knows about the special love I have for my brother. That love is best described in John 15:13, "Greater love has no one than this, that one lay down his life for his friends."

I thank my husband, Larry, for his encouragement to not give up; and for all the times he didn't complain with the twice baked leftovers during the process of deadlines which had to be met. The greatest thanks go to you for sharing me with my computer until its completion.

Lastly, I thank you, the reader, for joining me in the next 70 days, to gaze at God and glance at all else.

fran miller
Memphis, TN
December 1999

Introduction

Have you heard the story about the farmer who brought his family to the big city for the first time? They walked into the lobby of the tallest building and saw something they had never seen before. Two steel doors opened. A very large elderly woman walked in and the door closed behind her. They stood and watched and a minute later, the doors opened and a beautiful young woman walked out. The farmer turned to his son and said, "Wait right here. I'm going to get your mom and run her through that thing!"

Isn't that about how easy and fast we all want to become spiritually mature? And isn't that about how easy and fast we want to complete something God has called us to do? Growing up in Christ and being faithful to finish something He has called you to do is a process – a day by day and step by step process. My growing up in Christ and the completion of this book are prime examples of the difference of wrong expectations and reality.

My wrong expectation of understanding the Scriptures was that it would become automatic after I was saved. I became a Christian at the age of 12, but it took me 20 years to really begin to grow spiritually because I was just going to Church to be fed His Word. I wasn't studying His Word for myself. The reality of understanding the Scriptures came when I learned to ask the Holy Spirit to teach me. I then began to understand the secret of living the abundant, victorious life that our Lord Jesus came to give us. The secret is the title of this book. When we Gaze at God instead of gazing at our circumstances or pain and sorrow, we can experience joy in the midst of pain just like Paul did in Acts 16. Paul had been beaten, thrown into a maximum-security cell, shackled, and yet he began a midnight worship service. Paul had learned that praising God did not depend on his circumstances. That's the reality I desire for me and for you.

My wrong expectation of completing this book in a short amount of time was also a hard lesson for me to learn. The birth of this book began five years ago! Several people began to ask me if I would write a book with biblical principles. The thought of me writing a book made me laugh. A few weeks later, someone asked me the same question right after I had taught Matthew 17, the miracle of the money in the mouth of the fish. God woke me up the next morning with excitement and a desire to write. God showed me from the miracle of Matthew 17, that He loves to perform the unlikely. I had many questions for Him and He gave me promises and encouraged me all along the way. I went to my sister's house in the mountains that summer to begin the book. I spent a week writing one page. I immediately thought this project was too hard, so I stopped. I didn't begin again for two years. That's called disobedience. But once I understood the reality of finishing this book would be a process, I knew I couldn't give up.

So, I give you two challenges today. First, determine that you will spend time alone with God and grow in learning to keep your gaze on Him and glance at all else. Second, determine to persevere in whatever God has called you to do. Don't give up even if it is hard and will be a long process. He will enable those He calls.

Here are a few suggestions for your daily reading:

1. **Pray before you start** and ask the LORD to speak to you through the Scriptures, illustrations, applications and/or principle. Notice that the name LORD is in all capitals in the journal suggestion each day. LORD in all caps in Scripture is the name Jehovah. Jehovah is always used of God in His personal relationship and involvement with man. The LORD wants to be personally involved with all you and I do. The greatest difference in God creating the plants, stars and animals and man is that He became personally, intimately involved with man.
2. **Expect** Him to speak to you.
3. As you read, **underline** a command you need to obey, a promise you need to claim, or any warning you need to heed.
4. **Journal** what stood out to you personally. You may give yourself permission not to share this book since it will have your personal thoughts and prayers.
5. **Write** the principle on an index card and carry it with you that day to remind you of what the LORD taught you. There are 70 days, but only 35 principles because I have used the same principle for two days in a row to show how a biblical principle can be seen in different Scriptures.
6. **Share** what you learned with one other person each day. This will help you retain life lessons and might help someone else at the same time. That's how God works.

Gaze at God
Glance at All Else

Day 1: 1 Samuel 17:4-9,45-49

Then a champion came out from the armies of the Philistines named Goliath, from Gath, whose height was six cubits and a span. And he had a bronze helmet on his head, and he was clothed with scale-armor which weighed five thousand shekels of bronze. He also had bronze greaves on his legs and a bronze javelin slung between his shoulders. And the shaft of his spear was like a weaver's beam, and the head of his spear weighed six hundred shekels of iron; his shield-carrier also walked before him. And he stood and shouted to the ranks of Israel, and said to them, "Why do you come out to draw up in battle array? Am I not the Philistine and you servants of Saul? Choose a man for yourselves and let him come down to me. If he is able to fight with me and kill me, then we will become your servants; but if I prevail against him and kill him, then you shall become our servants and serve us."…Then David said to the Philistine, "You come to me with a sword, a spear, and a javelin, but I come to you in the name of the LORD of hosts, the God of the armies of Israel, whom you have taunted. This day the LORD will deliver you up into my hands, and I will strike you down and remove your head from you. And I will give the dead bodies of the army of the Philistines this day to the birds of the sky and the wild beasts of the earth, that all the earth may know that there is a God in Israel, and that all this assembly may know that the LORD does not deliver by sword or by spear; for the battle is the LORD's and He will give you into our hands." Then it happened when the Philistine rose and came and drew near to meet David, that David ran quickly toward the battle line to meet the Philistine. **And David put his hand into his bag and took from it a stone and slung it, and struck the Philistine on his forehead. And the stone sank into his forehead, so that he fell on his face to the ground.**

When David was just a boy, he was a shepherd…and being a shepherd meant two things. First, it meant that you would have problems with wild animals attacking your herd. Second, tending sheep meant that you would spend a great deal of time alone. In the fields, God was preparing David to fight an even bigger problem – Goliath. It was during this time that God was training David to depend on Him.

David heard that this towering man dressed with 200 pounds of armor had been taunting the armies of the living God, so he came to fight him.

What chance did David have against such a giant? In verse 47, we find the answer: "the battle is the LORD's." David discovered a great truth from God during all that time he was a shepherd boy, alone with the living God. He learned that in every problem he faced, God stood ready to help him handle it. David knew his God was bigger than any problem. David knew that giants do reside, but they don't have to rule.

Illustration

Maybe it has happened to you before. You are sound asleep and the phone rings at 2:00 a.m. Your heart races as you begin to guess who it is and what has happened. Good news usually doesn't come at that hour. At 2:00 a.m., it's usually a giant you are facing.

And with every problem, we need to remember that giants do exist today. Giants with names like loneliness, weariness, misunderstanding, rejection, disappointment, resentment, and what about that big giant, "what if?" What if…I make the wrong decision? What if…I fail at my job? What if…the operation doesn't work?

Giants do reside, but they don't have to rule.

Your giant may not be my giant. But whatever giant you are facing – it doesn't have to rule. What we need to do is to turn over our giants to the giant slayer—the living LORD.

Journal

What has the LORD highlighted to you through today's reading?

Giants can be loneliness, rejection, disappointment and what if. What if seems like a big giant to me at this time. He is with me acting as my giant and making my giants much easier knowing I give them to him to carry me were he wants me to be.

Application

Will you approach your giant with faith today, not fear? Is your giant controlling you? To be in control of your giant, would you do the following three things? First, name your giant. Second, face your giant. That means to compare the size and power of your giant next to the size and power of the LORD. Third, fight your giant. You fight by putting on the armor of God (Ephesians 6:10-20), and trusting Him to work in your behalf. Knowing He is in charge makes all the difference! Remember that you, not your giant, have promises from God.

Principle

Giants reside – but don't have to rule.

Day 2: Apply this principle to your life

Giants reside–but don't have to rule.

Then the LORD spoke to Moses saying, "Send out for yourself men so that they may spy out the land of Canaan, which I am going to give to the sons of Israel; you shall send a man from each of their fathers' tribes, every one a leader among them." Numbers 13:1-2

What promise did God make to Moses? *Give Canaan land to Israel*

Isn't it interesting that God knew what would happen, and He wanted to show His plan to them? Jeremiah 29:11 says, "'For I know the plans that I have for you,' declares the LORD, 'plans for welfare and not for calamity, to give you a future and a hope.'" But He tells us in the next verse that we are to be involved.

Jeremiah 29:12 says, "Then you will call upon Me and come and pray to Me, and I will listen to you."

It was God's idea for Moses to send 12 men to spy out the condition of the land.

> *When Moses sent them to spy out the land of Canaan, he said to them, "Go up there into the Negev; then go up into the hill country. And see what the land is like, and whether the people who live in it are strong or weak, whether they are few or many. And how is the land in which they live, is it good or bad? And how are the cities in which they live, are they like open camps or with fortifications? And how is the land, is it fat or lean? Are there trees in it or not? Make an effort then to get some of the fruit of the land." Now the time was the time of the first ripe grapes. So they went up and spied out the land.*   Numbers 13:17-21

What were these 12 men told to bring back? *Grapes; Fruit of the land*

Numbers 13:23 tell us that the grapes they brought back were so large they had to carry them on a pole between two men.

> *When they returned from spying out the land, at the end of forty days, they proceeded to come to Moses and Aaron and to all the congregation of the sons of Israel in the wilderness of Paran, at Kadesh; and they brought back word to them and to all the congregation and showed them the fruit of the land. Thus they told him, and said, "We went in to the land where you sent us; and it certainly does flow with milk and honey, and this is its fruit. Nevertheless, the people who live in the land are strong, and the cities are fortified and very large; and moreover, we saw the descendants of Anak there." Then Caleb quieted the people before Moses,*

and said, "We should by all means go up and take possession of it, for we shall surely overcome it." But the men who had gone up with him said, "We are not able to go up against the people, for they are too strong for us." Numbers 13:25-28,30-31

Did Caleb stand with the majority or the minority? _____

Caleb didn't succumb to the giant of unpopularity. How could Caleb be so bold to take a stand against the crowd? Caleb knew that truth can't be measured by numbers, but by what the Lord says. Did you notice that there are no conflicting reports about the land, but only the advice about what should be done? Fear can keep us from claiming our possessions.

And Joshua the son of Nun and Caleb the son of Jephunneh, of those who had spied out the land, tore their clothes; and they spoke to all the congregation of the sons of Israel, saying, "The land which we passed through to spy out is an exceedingly good land. If the LORD is pleased with us, then He will bring us into this land, and give it to us—a land which flows with milk and honey. Only do not rebel against the LORD; and do not fear the people of the land, for they shall be our prey. Their protection has been removed from them, and the LORD is with us; do not fear them." Numbers 14:6-9

Who were the two spies that wanted to go in and possess the land? Who gave them the victory? Where was Joshua and Caleb's focus?

_____

Twelve men were sent out to spy the land and the report came back that the land was great, but there were giant men there. There were also giant grapes, for it took two men to carry one cluster of grapes. Ten of the twelve spies saw only obstacles. Two saw opportunities. Ten gazed at the obstacles and responded with fear because they didn't trust God. Two of them glanced at the obstacles, gazed at God and responded with faith because they knew God had called them to take possession of the land.

Sometimes we gaze where we should be glancing and glance where we should be gazing. When we gaze at our giants of fear and unbelief, our difficulties are magnified. Then we are tempted to rationalize that God can't be trusted. We begin to focus on the "we are not able," rather than focus on the God Who is able.

Journal

What positive characteristics of God can overcome the negative fears of your heart?

_____

_____

Day 3: James 3:1-12

Let not many of you become teachers, my brethren, knowing that as such we shall incur a stricter judgment. For we all stumble in many ways. If anyone does not stumble in what he says, he is a perfect man, able to bridle the whole body as well. Now if we put the bits into the horses' mouths so that they may obey us, we direct their entire body as well. Behold, the ships also, though they are so great and are driven by strong winds, are still directed by a very small rudder, wherever the inclination of the pilot desires. **So also the tongue is a small part of the body, and yet it boasts of great things. Behold, how great a forest is set aflame by such a small fire!** *And the tongue is a fire, the very world of iniquity; the tongue is set among our members as that which defiles the entire body, and sets on fire the course of our life, and is set on fire by hell. For every species of beasts and birds, of reptiles and creatures of the sea, is tamed, and has been tamed by the human race. But no one can tame the tongue; it is a restless evil and full of deadly poison. With it we bless our* Lord *and Father; and with it we curse men, who have been made in the likeness of God; from the same mouth come both blessing and cursing. My brethren, these things ought not to be this way. Does a fountain send out from the same opening both fresh and bitter water? Can a fig tree, my brethren, produce olives, or a vine produce figs? Neither can salt water produce fresh.*

The people in James' day seemed to be having trouble with their tongues. Imagine that! Yet, he says in verse 8 that nobody can tame the tongue. So, if they couldn't tame their tongues, what could they do? What was their real problem? Matthew 12:34b says it is a heart problem: "For the mouth speaks out of that which fills the heart." Matthew 15:18 adds: "But the things that proceed out of the mouth come from the heart, and those defile the man."

The Christians then needed a reminder: submission of the heart changes the condition of the tongue. Before they opened their mouths, they needed to ask one question: who am I allowing to be in control of my heart, and thus, my words? Good question for us as well!

Illustration

It takes a baby two years to learn to talk and 50 years to try to keep their mouth shut. When I heard certain words come out of my five-year-old's mouth, I took her into the bathroom and wiped a bar of soap across her tongue. I'm not sure I would do that today, but it makes a good point.

We need to stop before speaking and ask: are my words going to bless or blast?

If what you are about to say would be put up on a big billboard, what would it advertise about the condition of your heart? Your mouth is the billboard of your heart. Do your words come from a submissive or a rebellious heart? Proverbs 18:21 says: "Death and life are in the power of the tongue." David, the psalmist, prayed in Psalm 141:3: "Set a guard over my mouth; keep watch over the doors of my lips."

In verse 5, we see that even though the tongue is a small part of the body, it has great influence. Our tongues can do as much damage to other people as a great fire did to Chicago. In 1871, the Great Chicago Fire started when Mrs. O'Leary was milking a cow in her barn. The cow kicked the lantern over and straw ignited. The blaze became so great, 17,500 people were left homeless–all because of one cow and one lantern. God says the tongue is like that. Small, but lethal.[1]

Application

Will you start the day by submitting your heart to Him and asking Him to guard your words today? Then, before you speak a word today, think if your words will bless or blast? What positive words need to be heard by your family, friends or coworkers this week?

Journal

What has the LORD highlighted to you through today's reading?

_____

_____

_____

_____

_____

_____

_____

_____

_____

_____

_____

Principle

Your mouth is the billboard of your heart.

Day 4: Apply this principle to your life
Your mouth is the billboard of your heart.

I was talking to a friend of mine whose husband is my dentist. I don't know how we got on this subject, but she taught me that we need not only to brush our teeth, but our tongues as well. Sometimes I think I need to have mine amputated! Have you ever said something and then were sick those words came from your mouth? I have. And I've also been sick from things that were said to me. So let's look at some words that are unwise and some that are wise.

Unwise Words:

A harsh word stirs up anger.   Proverbs 15:1b

"Your words have been arrogant against Me," says the LORD. "Yet you say, 'What have we spoken against Thee?'"   Malachi 3:13

And in their greed they will exploit you with false words; their judgment from long ago is not idle, and their destruction is not asleep.   2 Peter 2:3

Better to live in a desert than with a quarrelsome and ill-tempered wife.   Proverbs 21:19 (NIV)

Wise Words:

This you know, my beloved brethren. But let everyone be quick to hear, slow to speak and slow to anger.   James 1:19

A gentle answer turns away wrath.   Proverbs 15:1a

The LORD God has given Me the tongue of disciples, that I may know how to sustain the weary one with a word. He awakens Me morning by morning, He awakens My ear to listen as a disciple.   Isaiah 50:4

A man has joy in an apt answer, and how delightful is a timely word!   Proverbs 15:23

Like apples of gold in settings of silver is a word spoken in right circumstances.   Proverbs 25:11

She opens her mouth in wisdom, and the teaching of kindness is on her tongue.   Proverbs 31:26

No man can tame the tongue without divine grace and assistance:

We can ask God to help us restrain our tongues.

Set a guard, O LORD, over my mouth; keep watch over the door of my lips.   Psalm 141:3

The one who guards his mouth preserves his life; the one who opens wide his lips comes to ruin.
Proverbs 13:3

He who guards his mouth and his tongue, guards his soul from troubles.
Proverbs 21:23

If anyone thinks himself to be religious, and yet does not bridle his tongue but deceives his own heart, this man's religion is worthless.
James 1:26

Journal

From today's Scriptures how do you want the LORD to help you control your tongue?

_____

_____

Day 5: Genesis 7:1-4; 8:1,15-16; 9:11-13

Then the LORD said to Noah, "Enter the ark, you and all your household; for you alone I have seen to be righteous before Me in this time. You shall take with you of every clean animal by sevens, a male and his female; and of the animals that are not clean two, a male and his female; also of the birds of the sky, by sevens, male and female, to keep offspring alive on the face of all the earth. For after seven more days, I will send rain on the earth forty days and forty nights; and I will blot out from the face of the land every living thing that I have made."...**But God remembered Noah and all the beasts and all the cattle that were with him in the ark; and God caused a wind to pass over the earth, and the water subsided** ...Then God spoke to Noah, saying, "Go out of the ark, you and your wife and your sons and your sons' wives with you...And I establish My covenant with you; and all flesh shall never again be cut off by the water of the flood, neither shall there again be a flood to destroy the earth." And God said, "This is the sign of the covenant which I am making between Me and you and every living creature that is with you, for all successive generations; I set My bow in the cloud, and it shall be for a sign of a covenant between Me and the earth."

Even though Noah was trusting, believing and obeying God, he still had to weather the storm for 40 days and nights. In Genesis 7:1-4, we read that the LORD commanded Noah to enter the ark. This is the last recorded time that God spoke to Noah until the flood receded. During the year of the flood, it seems that God is silent. Noah couldn't row or stop the storm or bail out. By faith, Noah waited for God to complete His purpose. Noah continued to trust God – even in the solitude of His stillness. Noah had walked with God; now he waited on God. No matter how black the storm, the light remains on the other side.

Illustration

I gathered my children together and headed off to the grocery store for the third time in one day. As soon as I pulled into the parking lot, I remembered I left my one-year-old at home taking a nap! If you are now asking me how in the world one might forget a baby, you aren't old enough or scattered enough...yet! And if you are still asking, I understand. I asked my Dad the same thing when he came home one day from the grocery store without my little brother. How can someone not remember his own child?

Unlike us, God never forgets His children and His timing is perfect. Isaiah 49:15-16 says, "I will not forget you. Behold, I have inscribed you on the palms of My hands."

When Genesis 8:1 points out that God remembered Noah, it doesn't mean He had forgotten Noah at all. It means that the time had now come for God to act. God was ready to change the circumstances. And the day is coming when He will reach down and touch you and your circumstances to change your life. And when He does, don't you want to look back and be able to say that you were faithful, whether in a storm, or in the solitude of His stillness?

Journal

What has the LORD highlighted to you through today's reading?

_____

_____

_____

_____

_____

_____

_____

_____

_____

_____

_____

_____

_____

_____

_____

_____

_____

_____

Application

Are you listening to God, obeying Him and trusting His timing in the midst of your storms? Can God trust you in days of His silence? Are you more preoccupied with being comfortable and successful than you are with being faithful?

Principle

God never forgets His children and His timing is perfect.

Day 6: Apply this principle to your life

God never forgets His children and His timing is perfect.

Do you know the difference between a turkey and an eagle? You can tell the difference when a storm comes up. The turkey puts his wings around his head, runs for cover and hopes the storm won't come near him. The eagle senses the storm, spreads his wings and lets the air current of the storm take him higher and higher above the storm. While the turkey is hiding during the storm, the eagle is soaring above it.

Are you a turkey waiting to become an eagle? _____

Surely there were times when Noah felt like a turkey, but as we read about his life in Genesis, we see that Noah was one who trusted in God and trusted in God's timing. It took Noah 120 years to build the boat that was one and a half times the size of a football field. Think about the kind of faith it would take to continue believing a flood was really going to come when in fact, they had never seen it rain.

Do you believe that God's timing is perfect? If you do, then why do you question when He hasn't answered your prayer?

_____

_____

_____

God's timing is probably one subject my youngest daughter could write about very easily. Many times she questioned His timing. But this particular day, something was different. Three of us - my daughter, my friend, and I were doing a Bible study at my house. At the end, we always shared prayer requests and then prayed. My daughter asked us to pray for God to bring the husband of His choice to her. Her request had been given before, but this time, it was a request that was willing to wait for the right one. The request was different because she was different. God had been doing a work in her heart and there was now a surrender of her will. You know the kind. The kind of surrender that makes the waiting easier and yet exciting – because you trust Him to answer and you trust His timing. "In the morning, O LORD, Thou wilt hear my voice; in the morning I will order my prayer to Thee and eagerly watch." (Psalm 5:3)

After praying together, I said to her that she never went anywhere but to work, home, church and my house. Then I said, "I guess He will have to bring him to you, so watch the door." She left and went to work. That very night, God brought him through the door of her workplace. They met, knew something was different and were married nine months later. I wish my son-in-law could tell you the whole story. He does a much better job of sharing it than I have. He says he found his "princess" and we say "thank you LORD for answered prayer."

Don't miss the object of the story. It's not that you can pray and your prince will knock at your door. The object is that when God is ready to move in your life, He will. Our part is to surrender our expectations to Him and trust God to give us what He sees is best for our life. If Noah could trust God for 120 years, we can too.

Below are some things to do and promises to claim while we're waiting. We need to remember that while we wait we are to keep on doing what He has already called us to do. Then use this time to allow Him to work on the other end of your request before the answer comes.

Therefore, return to your God, observe kindness and justice, and wait for your God continually. *Hosea 12:6*

Wait for the LORD; be strong, and let your heart take courage; yes, wait for the LORD. *Psalm 27:14*

My soul, wait in silence for God only, for my hope is from Him. He only is my rock and my salvation, my stronghold; I shall not be shaken. *Psalm 62:5-6*

O LORD, be gracious to us; we have waited for Thee. Be Thou their strength every morning, our salvation also in the time of distress. *Isaiah 33:2*

I am weary with my crying; my throat is parched; my eyes fail while I wait for my God. *Psalm 69:3*

Yet those who wait for the LORD will gain new strength; they will mount up with wings like eagles, they will run and not get tired, they will walk and not become weary. *Isaiah 40:31*

Journal

What answered prayer are you waiting for? How can you serve God while you wait?

_____

_____

_____

_____

_____

_____

Day 7: Acts 10:1-9, 17-23

Now there was a certain man at Caesarea named Cornelius, a centurion of what was called the Italian cohort, a devout man, and one who feared God with all his household, and gave many alms to the Jewish people, and prayed to God continually. About the ninth hour of the day he clearly saw in a vision an angel of God who had just come in to him, and said to him, "Cornelius!" And fixing his gaze upon him and being much alarmed, he said, "What is it, LORD?" And he said to him, "Your prayers and alms have ascended as a memorial before God. And now dispatch some men to Joppa, and send for a man named Simon, who is also called Peter; he is staying with a certain tanner named Simon, whose house is by the sea." And when the angel who was speaking to him had departed, he summoned two of his servants and a devout soldier of those who were in constant attendance upon him, and after he had explained everything to them, he sent them to Joppa.

And on the next day, as they were on their way, and approaching the city, Peter went up on the housetop about the sixth hour to pray…Now while

Peter was greatly perplexed in mind as to what the vision which he had seen might be, behold, the men who had been sent by Cornelius, having asked directions for Simon's house, appeared at the gate; and calling out, they were asking whether Simon, who was also called Peter, was staying there. **And while Peter was reflecting on the vision, the Spirit said to him, "Behold, three men are looking for you. But arise, go downstairs, and accompany them without misgivings; for I have sent them Myself."** *And Peter went down to the men and said, "Behold, I am the one you are looking for; what is the reason for which you have come?" And they said, "Cornelius, a centurion, a righteous and God-fearing man well spoken of by the entire nation of the Jews, was divinely directed by a holy angel to send for you to come to his house and hear a message from you." And so he invited them in and gave them lodging.*

And on the next day he arose and went away with them, and some of the brethren from Joppa accompanied him.

Cornelius, a Roman officer, was in Caesarea. Peter was staying in Joppa, about 30 miles away. God was working in both of their lives at the same time. Cornelius was not only an important man in command of 100 men, he was also a religious man. Being important and religious doesn't make one a believer. As far as Cornelius understood, he was a God-fearing man, but had no personal relationship with the Lord. So God gave Cornelius a vision and commanded him to send some men to Joppa for a man named Peter. And at the same time, God was giving Peter a vision that they were coming. In this Scripture, we see God was working behind the scenes in both of their lives. He was preparing Peter to share Christ with Cornelius, and preparing Cornelius to receive Christ.

Illustration

Our son came home after backpacking in Europe and was living with us for a short time. He found an apartment and asked if I would decorate it before he moved in. I had three weeks to shop and gather things together to decorate. He had taken some great pictures on his trip, so I took them to have them enlarged. As I was checking out, the young man who was helping me asked me what I was going to do with all the pictures. I explained I would dry mount them to boards and use them to decorate my son's apartment. With a priceless expression on his face, he asked me if my son knew what I was doing. I responded, "No, he has no idea how I am decorating. He just knows I'm working on it and doesn't want to see it until the day he moves in."

Wouldn't it be great if we could go through life with the assurance that someone is always working behind the scenes for us? Well, carry this with you all day: there is Someone! His name is Jesus and He is always working behind the scenes. He is doing it today in your life; your child's life; in your workplace; in that lost soul for whom you have been praying for so long.

That's His job! That's His joy! Who knows, maybe He will soon show you what He has been doing. Until then, keep believing. Keep praying. Keep watching.

Journal

What has the LORD highlighted to you through today's reading?

_____
_____
_____
_____
_____
_____

Application

How can you be more like Cornelius and Peter? Are you never, often, or always surprised to find out that God has been preparing you for something that He wants you to do? Then, are you equally surprised when you find out that He was working behind the scenes on the other end? Will you thank Him now for what He is doing behind the scenes, even if you can't see anything quite yet? Would you tell Him now how much you are encouraged because He's working in your loved ones' lives right now?

Principle

God is always working behind the scenes.

Day 8: Apply this principle to your life

God is always working behind the scenes.

A pastor was standing at the door greeting people after the service. A young boy was walking out with his family when the pastor decided to ask him some questions to determine just how much he had learned. He said, "Young man, if you can tell me something that God can do, I'll give you a big shiny apple." Thoughtfully the boy replied, "Sir, if you can tell me something God can't do, I'll give you a whole box of apples." [2]

Now that's the kind of faith we need today. When we read the Scripture from yesterday's reading, we understand how God was working "back then." But when we try to apply His sovereign ways to our own life, it gets a little harder. Hebrews 13:8 tell us that God is always the same: "Jesus Christ is the same yesterday and today, yes and forever."

All of our thoughts and actions are before Him. That is how He can work behind the scenes in so many people's lives at the same time. Psalm 139 is a meditation on God's omnipresence (He is everywhere) and God's omniscience (He knows all things). Let's be aware of God's loving knowledge of and caring control over our lives as we read some of the verses from this Psalm.

> O LORD, You have searched me and You know me. You know when I sit and when I rise; You perceive my thoughts from afar. You discern my going out and my lying down; You are familiar with all my ways. Before a word is on my tongue You know it completely, O LORD. You hem me in - behind and before; You have laid Your hand upon me. Such knowledge is too wonderful for me, too lofty for me to attain. *Psalm 139:1-6 (NIV)*

> For You created my inmost being; You knit me together in my mother's womb. I praise You because I am fearfully and wonderfully made; Your works are wonderful, I know that full well. My frame was not hidden from You when I was made in the secret place. When I was woven together in the depths of the earth, your eyes saw my unformed body. All the days ordained for me were written in your book before one of them came to be. *Psalm 139:13-16 (NIV)*

From Psalm 139:1-6, name all the different things that David said God knew about him?

_____

_____

_____

From verse 14, what was David praising God for? _____

> *From His dwelling place He looks out on all the inhabitants of the earth.*
>
> Psalm 33:14

> *The eyes of the LORD are in every place.*   Proverbs 15:3a

How much can the LORD see at once? _____

> *Therefore do not be like them; for your Father knows what you need,*
> *before you ask Him.*
>
> Matthew 6:8

The LORD has already gone before you in knowing what you need before you even ask Him. If He doesn't give you what you have asked for, it is because He knows you don't need it and it's not for your own good. Trust that He goes before you and is always working behind the scenes, even if you can't see the outcome.

Journal

Write about any of today's reading which has helped to encourage you personally today.

_____

_____

_____

_____

_____

_____

_____

_____

_____

_____

_____

_____

_____

_____

Day 9: 1 Corinthians 9:11-12,24-27

*If we sowed spiritual things in you, is it too much if we should reap material things from you? If others share the right over you, do we not more? Nevertheless, we did not use this right, but we endure all things, that we may cause no hindrance to the gospel of Christ...Do you not know that those who run in a race all run, but only one receives the prize? Run in such a way that you may win. **And everyone who competes in the games exercises self-control in all things.** They then do it to receive a perishable wreath, but we an imperishable. Therefore I run in such a way, as not without aim; I box in such a way, as not beating the air; but I buffet my body and make it my slave, lest possibly, after I have preached to others, I myself should be disqualified.*

As we read about Paul's life and ministry, we wonder how he was able to lead such a disciplined life. As founder of the church in Corinth, Paul had a right to receive financial support from them. But he chose not to. Verse 12 explains that Paul didn't want anything to hinder the spread of God's Word. He may have thought some would think he was just out for their money.

No one runs a race without expecting to win. Paul's goal was to win a prize to present the day he would stand face to face with the Lord Jesus at the Judgement Seat. He knew how important discipline was to achieving his goal. He also realized he must discipline his mind as well as his body. The last three verses of chapter 9 tell us that Paul knew what it was like to run a race: "Everyone who competes in the games goes into strict training. They do it to get a crown that will not last; but we do it to get a crown that will last forever. Therefore, I do not run like a man running aimlessly; I do not fight like a man beating the air. No, I beat my body and make it my slave so that after I have preached to others, I myself will not be disqualified for the prize." (NIV)

Life is a race that demands discipline.

Illustration

We went to see the production *Lord of the Dance*. The young dancers could move their feet faster than anyone I have ever seen. And they danced for an hour and a half. I thought that maybe I could do it if I practiced a few weeks. When intermission came, we walked up the stairs to the roof and I could hardly breathe. It impressed me to think of all the discipline it takes to be able to dance that fast and that long.

It also made me think how often we want to intimately know God and His Word with great understanding but without disciplining ourselves to spend time studying and praying. I look at my spiritual mentors and want to know Him as they do. Then I remember what Ray Stedman told me: "If you discipline yourself to study God's Word for as long as I have, you will know as much as I do when you are my age." I do know Jesus better today than I did last month. And I pray I will be faithful to know Him even better next month.

Journal

What has the LORD highlighted to you through today's reading?

_____

_____

_____

_____

_____

_____

_____

_____

_____

_____

_____

_____

_____

_____

_____

_____

_____

Application

How much time per day do you set aside to read His Word? What would you be willing to lay aside so you would have more time for Him to speak directly to your heart through His Word? Since there is no victory without discipline and sacrifice, what will you do to win the race? What do you expect your prize to be at the end of the race: is winning for the glory of God enough for you?

Principle

Life is a race that demands discipline.

Day 10: *Apply this principle to your life*

Life is a race that demands discipline.

Last week when I was walking in the park, I stopped to watch some girls race. They were running toward the finish line where their coach was standing. I was amazed at how fast they ran. Their coach had a time watch and after the race, he spoke to each one of them separately. I guess he was telling them their time. All of them were smiling from ear to ear. From the look on the coach's face, he was pleased too. I wonder, will that be what it will be like when we get Home? Will we run toward the Father and be greeted with a "well done, my good and faithful servant?" (Matthew 25:21) We will spend eternity realizing that all the discipline and sacrifice were worth it, because it made us look more like Him, and that pleases the Father.

When my children played any kind of sports, they had to have self-discipline in order to train. We as Christians also need self-discipline.

Paul says in 2 Timothy 1:7, " For God has not given us a spirit of timidity, but of power and love and discipline." We must appropriate that gift so we can run the race well.

This spiritual race we are in also demands self-control. I memorized the fruit of the Spirit in Galatians 5:22-23, years ago, but out of the 9 fruit, guess which one I always forgot? Self-control! Could that be because I was having a little trouble in that area? You don't have to answer that question! Maybe a little more self-control would help me run the race better.

Grade yourself from the following verses; then talk to Him about it.

Therefore, prepare your minds for action; be self-controlled; set your hope fully on the grace to be given you when Jesus Christ is revealed.

1 Peter 1:13 (NIV)

We are commanded to be self-controlled. Knowing that we will meet Christ should be enough motive to work on our self-control.

Now for this very reason also, applying all diligence, in your faith supply moral excellence, and in your moral excellence, knowledge; and in your knowledge, self-control, and in your self-control, perseverance, and in your perseverance, godliness.

2 Peter 1:5-6

We are to be diligent in developing self-control.

> *Like a city that is broken into and without walls is a man who has no control over his spirit.*   Proverbs 25:28

Without walls around the city to protect them, they were vulnerable to attack. Without self-control, we too are open for all kinds of trouble.

> *Therefore, since we have so great a cloud of witnesses surrounding us, let us also lay aside every encumbrance, and the sin which so easily entangles us, and let us run with endurance the race that is set before us, fixing our eyes on Jesus, the author and perfecter of faith, who for the joy set before Him endured the cross, despising the shame, and has sat down at the right hand of the throne of God.*   Hebrews 12:1-2

May we run with _____ fixing our eyes on _____ the _____ and perfecter of our faith.

Journal

Use any part of today's reading that encourages you to ask God to help you have more discipline in your weakest area of self-control.

_____

_____

_____

_____

_____

_____

_____

_____

_____

_____

_____

_____

_____

_____

Day 11: Psalm 90:1-14

A Prayer of Moses the man of God. LORD, Thou hast been our dwelling place in all generations. Before the mountains were born, Or Thou didst give birth to the earth and the world, Even from everlasting to everlasting, Thou art God. Thou dost turn man back into dust, And dost say, "Return, O children of men." For a thousand years in Thy sight Are like yesterday when it passes by, Or as a watch in the night. Thou hast swept them away like a flood, they fall asleep; In the morning they are like grass which sprouts anew. In the morning it flourishes, and sprouts anew; Toward evening it fades, and withers away. For we have been consumed by Thine anger, And by Thy wrath we have been dismayed. Thou hast placed our iniquities before Thee, Our secret sins in the light of Thy presence. For all our days have declined in Thy fury; We have finished our years like a sigh. As for the days of our life, they contain seventy years, Or if due to strength, eighty years, Yet their pride is but labor and sorrow; For soon it is gone and we fly away. Who understands the power of Thine anger, And Thy fury, according to the fear that is due Thee? **So teach us to number our days, That we may present to Thee a heart of wisdom.** *Do return, O LORD; how long will it be? And be sorry for Thy servants.* **O satisfy us in the morning with Thy lovingkindness, That we may sing for joy and be glad all our days.**

This Psalm is a prayer from the heart of Moses, who asked the LORD for two things: to teach us to use our time wisely, and to find our greatest satisfaction in Him. Moses knew that his days on earth were limited, and he wanted to spend time being satisfied and completely fulfilled in the everlasting, satisfying God.

Moses teaches us in Psalm 90:12 that we are to number our days. William Marston asked 3,000 persons, "What have you to live for?" He was shocked to find that 94 percent were simply enduring today to get to tomorrow. They would describe this as waiting for "something" to happen – waiting for children to grow up and leave home, waiting for next year, waiting for another time to take a long-dreamed trip, waiting for tomorrow. They were all waiting without realizing that all anyone ever has is today because yesterday is gone and tomorrow hasn't come. How sad these people were enduring today to get to tomorrow! Yet, what is even sadder, I too have spent time doing that same thing. Have you? [3]

Illustration

As I am writing this, I am sitting by the ocean. I'm on one of those trips where everyone is oblivious to what time it is, since there is no time schedule. As I meditated on this Psalm, you would think it would motivate me to go get my watch and spend some time doing something productive for God. Most of us are "doing" people. But Moses' walk with God teaches that truly being with Him is the most active thing that we can do. And Moses was very active about being with God. In spending so much intimate time together, one of the greatest lessons Moses learned was finding his satisfaction in Him – not in leading the people, owning the fastest camel, or discovering a new well, but finding satisfaction in the Wellspring of Life, God Himself.

Today verse 14 is my prayer for you and for me: "O satisfy us in the morning with Thy lovingkindness, that we may sing for joy and be glad all our days." For surely, being joyful in God is one of the greatest pleasures we can bring to Him.

Journal

What has the LORD highlighted to you through today's reading?

_____

_____

_____

_____

_____

_____

_____

_____

_____

_____

_____

_____

Application

Are you using your time wisely? Where do you find your greatest satisfaction? What steps will you take in order to find your satisfaction in your relationship with God rather than in the things of the world? Will you begin now committing this verse to memory and using it as part of your daily prayer? (Be sure to change the pronoun to refer to yourself.) "O satisfy _____ in the morning with Thy lovingkindness, that _____ may sing for joy and be glad all _____ days." Psalm 90:14

Principle

Finding your satisfaction in God is one of the greatest pleasures you bring to Him.

Day 12: Apply this principle to your life

Finding your satisfaction in God
is one of the greatest pleasures you bring to Him.

Have you ever received a dozen red roses with a card attached saying, "My beloved, I'm sending these roses to you because I feel like it's my duty since it is your birthday." If I did, it would not bring me pleasure. I wonder if that is how God feels when we come to Him and follow Him only out of duty.

John Piper wrote a book called *Desiring God*. His aim in the book is to persuade readers that the chief end of man is to glorify God **by** enjoying Him forever. What a great way to walk with Him. To desire to glorify Him in all we do because we enjoy Him should be our life's goal.

The purpose of today's reading is for us to explore some familiar Scriptures that will help us desire to find our satisfaction in Him.

We can find satisfaction and joy in:

The strength of the LORD

> *Whom have I in heaven but Thee? And besides Thee, I desire nothing on earth. My flesh and my heart may fail, but God is the strength of my heart and my portion forever.* Psalm 73:25-26

The beauty of the LORD

> *One thing I have asked from the LORD, that I shall seek: That I may dwell in the house of the LORD all the days of my life, to behold the beauty of the LORD, and to meditate in His temple.* Psalm 27:4

Our experiences with the LORD

> *O taste and see that the LORD is good; how blessed is the man who takes refuge in Him!* Psalm 34:8

Our listening to the LORD

> *How sweet are Thy words to my taste! Yes, sweeter than honey to my mouth!* Psalm 119:103

> *Thou wilt make known to me the path of life; In Thy presence is fullness of joy; In Thy right hand there are pleasures forever.* Psalm 16:11

Our prayer time with the LORD

> *Then I will go to the altar of God, to God my exceeding joy; And upon the lyre I shall praise Thee, O God, my God.* Psalm 43:4

Our nearness to the LORD

> *They delight in the nearness of God.*   Isaiah 58:2c

Our praising the LORD

> *I will bless the LORD at all times; His praise shall continually be in my mouth. My soul shall make its boast in the LORD; the humble shall hear it and rejoice. O magnify the LORD with me, and let us exalt His name together.*   Psalm 34:1-3

> *When I consider Thy heavens, the work of Thy fingers, the moon and the stars, which Thou hast ordained; what is man, that Thou dost take thought of him? And the son of man, that Thou dost care for him? Yet Thou hast made him a little lower than God, and dost crown him with glory and majesty! Thou dost make him to rule over the works of Thy hands; Thou hast put all things under his feet, all sheep and oxen, and also the beasts of the field, the birds of the heavens, and the fish of the sea, whatever passes through the paths of the seas. O LORD, our Lord, how majestic is Thy name in all the earth!*   Psalm 8:3-9

Journal

Use any of today's Scriptures that will help you find your satisfaction in Him. This is one of the greatest pleasures we bring to Him.

_____

_____

_____

_____

_____

_____

_____

_____

_____

_____

_____

_____

Day 13: Genesis 1:1-16

In the beginning God created the heavens and the earth. *And the earth was formless and void, and darkness was over the surface of the deep; and the Spirit of God was moving over the surface of the waters. Then God said, "Let there be light"; and there was light. And God saw that the light was good; and God separated the light from the darkness. And God called the light day, and the darkness He called night. And there was evening and there was morning, one day.*

Then God said, "Let there be an expanse in the midst of the waters, and let it separate the waters from the waters." And God made the expanse, and separated the waters which were below the expanse from the waters which were above the expanse; and it was so. And God called the expanse heaven. And there was evening and there was morning, a second day.

Then God said, "Let the waters below the heavens be gathered into one place, and let the dry land appear"; and it was so. And God called the dry land earth, and the gathering of the waters He called seas; and God saw that it was good. Then God said, "Let the earth sprout vegetation, plants yielding seed, and fruit trees bearing fruit after their kind, with seed in them, on the earth"; and it was so. And the earth brought forth vegetation, plants yielding seed after their kind, and trees bearing fruit, with seed in them, after their kind; and God saw that it was good. And there was evening and there was morning, a third day.

Then God said, "Let there be lights in the expanse of the heavens to separate the day from the night, and let them be for signs, and for seasons, and for days and years; and let them be for lights in the expanse of the heavens to give light on the earth"; and it was so. And God made the two great lights, the greater light to govern the day, and the lesser light to govern the night; He made the stars also.

The word for Genesis in the Greek means "beginning." Genesis gives the beginning of all except God. Even though this may be the most memorized verse in Scripture, it is probably the most questioned. How could there be no beginning for God? And how could we possibly understand that He created something out of nothing? How long did it take God to create the heavens and the earth? Our journey in God's Word begins with a test of faith.

The important thing is not how He created or how long it took Him. The important thing is that God did create the universe. And when we come to know the power of His Word, we can stand on this truth. Then, when we pass this first step of faith, we will begin to depend on God, who is greater than anything else in your life and mine.

Illustration

Have you ever done a school science project on the solar system? Out of all the projects that I have done, that is the one I remember the most. Here are some facts to show the magnitude of the heavens that God created. Our galaxy, the Milky Way, has over 400 billion stars. The Milky Way is only one among billions of galaxies in the known universe. Did you know that it would take 100,000 years for a beam of light, which travels 700 million miles per hour, to travel the length of our galaxy? When we think about God creating all this, we can understand that nothing is too large for Him. "Is anything too difficult for the LORD?" (Genesis 18:14a)

God also created the earth. Compared to the heavens, earth is small. Did you know that if the sun were hollow, hundreds of thousands of earths could fit inside? That tells me that God is involved with the small things, too. The smallest insect He created is made up of millions of living cells. There are some 75 trillion such cells in the body of an average person. God even created a sponge-like pad between a woodpecker's beak and head so when he drills a hole, he won't knock himself out! Nothing is too small for God to handle.

Journal

What has the LORD highlighted to you through today's reading?

_____

_____

_____

_____

_____

_____

_____

_____

Application

How big is your God? Is there anything too big or too small in your life that He cannot handle? Would you spend this day trusting that even if your financial situation, work situation, time schedule, health or decisions are greater than you are, they are not greater than God! He cares about every big and small detail in your life.

Principle

God is greater than anything in your life.

27

Day 14: Apply this principle to your life

God is greater than anything in your life.

Genesis 1:6-8 tells what God did on the second day of creation. He separated the waters. Earth was covered by water until God lifted the water to create atmosphere. Water is extremely dense and weighty. Carrying a pitcher of water gives a little hint of its weight, but getting slammed to the ocean floor by getting knocked off a raft really reveals the pressure of water. That happened to me and as I was struggling to swim to the surface, I realized there was nothing I could do until the pressure of that wave had moved forward. I was under too much pressure.

Are you under a lot of pressure right now? _____

Where is it coming from? _____

Is it too much for you? _____

God's power lifted billions of tons of water. All God did was speak and it was so. God can lift the pressure from your life. The circumstances may remain, but He can lift the pressure from your mind and heart. God is greater than the pressures in your life.

On the third day of creation, Genesis 1:9-13 tells us that God gathered all the water below the heavens into one place. Until the third day, man would have had to be a fish to live. Apparently, the earth was still covered with water. So God called the water into one place. Proverbs 8:29 says, "When He set for the sea its boundary, so that the water should not transgress His command, when He marked out the foundations of the earth."

God set boundaries for our good. The next time you are sitting by the ocean, reading a great book, and the water rolls almost to you, you will be thankful God created its boundaries. My aunt told me when I was a little girl that I was not to play in the field where there were some bulls. I was glad I obeyed those boundaries when I saw my friend climb the fence, only to make it out within a hair of getting hit by a bull. We are His children and God's greatness gives us boundaries because He foresees any danger ahead.

How and why are you grateful for the boundaries He has set for you throughout His Word?

_____

_____

_____

God's greatness:

> For great is the LORD, and greatly to be praised; He also is to be feared
> above all gods.   *1 Chronicles 16:25*

> Thine, O LORD, is the greatness and the power and the glory and the
> victory and the majesty, indeed everything that is in the heavens and the
> earth; Thine is the dominion, O LORD, and Thou dost exalt Thyself as
> head over all.   *1 Chronicles 29:11*

> Behold, let me tell you, you are not right in this, for God is greater than
> man.   *Job 33:12*

> For Thou art great and doest wondrous deeds; Thou alone art God.
>   *Psalm 86:10*

> Great is the LORD, and highly to be praised; and His greatness is
> unsearchable.   *Psalm 145:3*

> Who made heaven and earth, the sea and all that is in them; Who keeps
> faith forever.   *Psalm 146:6*

> Great is our LORD, and abundant in strength; His understanding is
> infinite.   *Psalm 147:5*

> Who has measured the waters in the hollow of His hand, and marked off
> the heavens by the span, and calculated the dust of the earth by the
> measure, and weighed the mountains in a balance, and the hills in a pair
> of scales? Who has directed the Spirit of the LORD, or as His counselor
> has informed Him?   *Isaiah 40:12-13*

Journal

List any pressures you are under today and then use any of today's Scriptures
that show how God is greater.

_____

_____

_____

_____

_____

_____

_____

Day 15: Jonah 1:1-4; 3:1-3; Psalm 139:9-10

The word of the LORD came to Jonah the son of Amittai saying, "Arise, go to Nineveh the great city, and cry against it, for their wickedness has come up before Me." But Jonah rose up to flee to Tarshish from the presence of the LORD. So he went down to Joppa, found a ship which was going to Tarshish, paid the fare, and went down into it to go with them to Tarshish from the presence of the LORD.

And the LORD hurled a great wind on the sea and there was a great storm on the sea so that the ship was about to break up.

Now the word of the LORD came to Jonah the second time, saying, "Arise, go to Nineveh the great city and proclaim to it the proclamation which I am going to tell you." So Jonah arose and went to Nineveh according to the word of the LORD. Now Nineveh was an exceedingly great city, a three days' walk.

If I take the wings of the dawn,
If I dwell in the remotest part
of the sea,
Even there Thy hand will lead me,
And Thy right hand will
lay hold of me.

A Sunday school teacher asked the class, "What do we learn from the story of Jonah and the whale?" A little boy raised his hand and said, "We learn that people make whales sick!" When we read this brief book in the Bible, we wonder why people don't make God so sick that He quits using imperfect people as channels of truth.

Yet, He still called His spotted, sanctified servant Jonah to go 500 miles to Nineveh to tell them that salvation is of the Lord. But Jonah headed 2000 miles in the opposite direction. Why? For a couple of reasons. Jonah feared for his life and he despised the Ninevites. The Ninevites were noted for their cruelty. When they captured a city, they would burn it, cut off the hands and ears of all the males, and then throw them into a pile to die. The children were burned at the stake. No wonder Jonah didn't want to go there.

But the book of Jonah is about more than an imperfect man. Jonah is a book about the patience of God. Psalm 103:8 says, "The LORD is compassionate and gracious, slow to anger and abounding in lovingkindness." It's about a God who died for all and desires all to know Him personally. It's about the power of God over circumstances, wind, fish, and the sea. It's about how the presence of God can be found even in the depths of the sea. (Read again Psalm 139:9-10). It's about the perseverance of God – Who never gives up on His plan, purpose and people. God will allow His servant to rebel and run away only so long before He intervenes and redirects his attention. God allows us to make U-turns and return to His plan for our lives.

Illustration

Two days ago, I received a phone call from my daughter, who is expecting their first child. She and her husband had just returned from the doctor's office with the exciting news that they were having a BOY. Well, if that wasn't enough news for this grandmother-to-be, I also learned of his name. Jonah Ryan. Of course our prayer for him is that he won't be rebellious. But as I focus on the book of Jonah, I see some wonderful characteristics we will pray for our Jonah to have. From Jonah 1:9 we pray he will be a godly man and fear God: "...I fear the LORD God of heaven who made the sea and the dry land." From 1:12 we pray he will be courageous and confess when he has sinned: "...pick me up and throw me into the sea. Then the sea will become calm for you, for I know that on account of me this great storm has come upon you." From 3:3 we pray that he will be obedient after being chastised and make a U-turn, returning to God: "So Jonah arose and went to Nineveh according to the word of the LORD."

Journal

What has the LORD highlighted to you through today's reading?

_____

_____

_____

_____

_____

_____

_____

_____

_____

_____

Application

What do you think God is trying to teach you through the story of Jonah? What are you running away from that God has called you to do or be? What characteristics of Jonah do you possess? Do you realize that even when our loved ones or we rebel against His will, He can use this time to teach great life lessons? Are you encouraged when you think how God has persevered and not given up on His plan, purpose or people?

Principle

God allows us to make U-turns and return to Him.

31

Day 16: Apply this principle to your life

God allows us to make U-turns and return to Him.

And Simon Peter answered and said, "Thou art the Christ, the Son of the living God." Matthew 16:16

Even though Peter believed in Jesus, his growing was a process.

Peter was weak at times:

> *And He came and found them sleeping, and said to Peter, "Simon, are you asleep? Could you not keep watch for one hour?"* Mark 14:37

Peter was self-seeking at times:

> *Then Peter answered and said to Him, "Behold, we have left everything and followed You; what then will there be for us?"* Matthew 19:27

Peter was impulsive at times:

> *While He was still speaking, behold, a multitude came, and the one called Judas, one of the twelve, was preceding them; and he approached Jesus to kiss Him. But Jesus said to him, "Judas, are you betraying the Son of Man with a kiss?" And when those who were around Him saw what was going to happen, they said, "Lord, shall we strike with the sword?" And a certain one of them struck the slave of the high priest and cut off his right ear. But Jesus answered and said, "Stop! No more of this." And He touched his ear and healed him.* Luke 22:47-51

Peter was a coward at times:

> *And seeing Peter warming himself, she looked at him, and said, "You, too, were with Jesus the Nazarene." But he denied it, saying, "I neither know nor understand what you are talking about." And he went out onto the porch. And the maid saw him, and began once more to say to the bystanders, "This is one of them!" But again he was denying it. And after a little while the bystanders were again saying to Peter, "Surely you are one of them, for you are a Galilean too." But he began to curse and swear, "I do not know this man you are talking about!"* Mark 14:67-71

Peter knew when he had been wrong:

> *And Peter remembered the word which Jesus had said, "Before a cock crows, you will deny Me three times." And he went out and wept bitterly.* Matthew 26:75

Peter was a man who belonged to the Lord and loved Him, but sometimes spoke without thinking, slept instead of watching and acted on impulse instead of waiting. Yet, the Lord always heard Peter's confession, forgave, and allowed Peter to make a U-turn and return to His plan. Peter must have been a very dizzy man! But after the resurrection of the Lord Jesus, Peter was the one Jesus singled out to hear that He was alive.

> *And looking up, they saw that the stone had been rolled away, although it was extremely large. And entering the tomb, they saw a young man sitting at the right, wearing a white robe; and they were amazed. And he said to them, 'Do not be amazed; you are looking for Jesus the Nazarene, who has been crucified. He has risen; He is not here; behold, here is the place where they laid Him. But go, tell His disciples and Peter, "He is going before you into Galilee; there you will see Him, just as He said to you."'*   *Mark 16:4-7*

Just like Jonah, Peter was allowed to make a U-turn and return to following God's plan for his life. Maybe you are rebelling against God and need to confess so you too can return to the right path of life.

> *For I confess my iniquity; I am full of anxiety because of my sin.*
>   *Psalm 38:18*

> *He who conceals his transgressions will not prosper, but he who confesses and forsakes them will find compassion.*   *Proverbs 28:13*

> *Therefore, confess your sins to one another, and pray for one another, so that you may be healed. The effective prayer of a righteous man can accomplish much.*   *James 5:16*

> *If we confess our sins, He is faithful and righteous to forgive us our sins and to cleanse us from all unrighteousness.*   *1 John 1:9*

Journal

Put your name in place of Peter's name and then confess where necessary, so you too may be restored to fellowship and return to His plan for your life.

_____

_____

_____

_____

_____

_____

Day 17: Acts 4:1-13,18-20

And as they were speaking to the people, the priests and the captain of the temple guard, and the Sadducees, came upon them, being greatly disturbed because they were teaching the people and proclaiming in Jesus the resurrection from the dead. And they laid hands on them, and put them in jail until the next day, for it was already evening. But many of those who had heard the message believed; and the number of the men came to be about five thousand.

And it came about on the next day, that their rulers and elders and scribes were gathered together in Jerusalem; and Annas the high priest was there, and Caiaphas and John and Alexander, and all who were of high-priestly descent. And when they had placed them in the center, they began to inquire, "By what power, or in what name, have you done this?" Then Peter, filled with the Holy Spirit, said to them, "Rulers and elders of the people, if we are on trial today for a benefit done to a sick man, as to how this man has been made well, let it be known to all of you, and to all the people of Israel, that by the name of Jesus Christ the Nazarene, whom you crucified, whom God raised from the dead— by this name this man stands here before you in good health. He is the STONE WHICH WAS REJECTED by you, THE BUILDERS, but WHICH BECAME THE VERY CORNER stone. And there is salvation in no one else; for there is no other name under heaven that has been given among men, by which we must be saved."

Now as they observed the confidence of Peter and John, and understood that they were uneducated and untrained men, they were marveling, and began to recognize them as having been with Jesus.

And when they had summoned them, they commanded them not to speak or teach at all in the name of Jesus. But Peter and John answered and said to them, "Whether it is right in the sight of God to give heed to you rather than to God, you be the judge; for we cannot stop speaking what we have seen and heard."

Here we have the testimony of Peter and John as they stood before a hostile audience. There were 71 people on the council and three-fourths of them were Sadducees. The Sadducees didn't believe in the resurrection or in the supernatural, and here were Peter and John sharing about both. They had just healed a crippled man and were preaching about the life, death, and resurrection of their Master and Savior, Jesus. So they were thrown into prison for doing a good thing. But they knew that everything could be taken away from them except their inner freedom through Christ.

They were commanded to stop speaking about Jesus, but they refused. We can find the continuation of this story in Acts 5. They were released for a short time, only to be arrested again. Peter and John used the power of the Holy Spirit to handle their persecution. They loved and honored Jesus so much that they were willing to suffer for His sake. In the process of suffering, their inner-man was being strengthened.

Illustration

Trials can be used to strengthen you and to draw you closer to Him. On the road of life, there are several pathways for handling persecution or opposition. Here are three paths from verses in Acts 4.

Verses 3-7: *Know that God is in control of all circumstances.* Did you notice that they didn't resist arrest? This persecution gave them an opportunity to preach to people they never would have been able to reach.

Verse 8: *Be filled with the Holy Spirit.* Because Peter was Spirit-filled, persecution drove him closer to the Lord. Being filled with the Holy Spirit allows Jesus to live His life through us. Some days we choose to be filled with anger and bitterness; others we choose to be like Peter and John, being filled with His character so that we may react to situations the way He would.

Verse 10: *Give God the glory for the victory.* In verse 7, the high officials asked Peter whose name or power he had used to heal the man (chapter 3). Peter gives all the glory to God. Peter agreed with David in Psalm 20:7, "Some boast in chariots, and some in horses; but we will boast in the name of the LORD our God." Psalm 145:11 says: "They shall speak of the glory of Thy kingdom, and talk of Thy power."

Journal

What has the LORD highlighted to you through today's reading?

_____

_____

_____

_____

_____

Application

How are you or a loved one being treated unjustly for doing a good thing? How has this experience drawn you closer to the Lord? How could it draw you farther away? When God displays His power in and through you, do you give glory to Him, or keep it for yourself? Will you spend more time with Jesus today so others will recognize you have been with Him? (Read again Acts 4:13)

Principle

Trials can be used to strengthen you and draw you closer to Him.

Day 18: Apply this principle to your life

Trials can be used to strengthen you
and draw you closer to Him.

Are there still people like Peter and John in our world today who will risk great pressures and trials in order to share Jesus with others? I received a letter from a friend who just graduated from college. She is in China as a missionary this year. Here is a small portion of her letter:

> Personally, the past few weeks have been a difficult learning process, as God has broken me and magnified my weaknesses, sins and distractions. I have also been broken physically as I have dealt with tonsillitis and some other minor problems. It has been hard, but I cannot stress enough how truly thankful I am to have gone through all of this. When we are flat on our faces before God and exposed for all that we really are, He is faithful to build us back up and to change us in the process. Even though we are shaken, He cannot be. Hudson Taylor summed up my sentiments exactly when he wrote that "difficulties afford a platform upon which He can show Himself. Without them we could never know how tender, faithful, and almighty our God is."

How wonderful to read such insight from someone so young. When I read what Hudson Taylor said, I was reminded of something I received in an e-mail. It is about how our difficulties afford a platform upon which He can show Himself. It was very encouraging to me. I pray it will encourage you too.

God said:

…If you never felt pain, then how would you know that I'm a Healer?

…If you never had a trial, how could you call yourself an overcomer?

…If you never felt sadness, how would you know that I'm a Comforter?

…If you knew all, how would you know that I would answer your questions?

…If you never had a problem, how would you know that I could solve them?

…If you never went through the fire, then how would you become pure?

…If you had all power, then how would you learn to depend on Me?

…If your life was perfect, then what would you need Me for?

Our Lord wants us to need Him and depend on Him. If we will, we will see the same results that we find in Romans 5:3,4:

We can rejoice, too, when we run into problems and trials, for we know that they are good for us—they help us learn to be patient. And patience develops strength of character in us and helps us trust God more each time we use it until finally our hope and faith are strong and steady. (TLB)

My husband has repeated this verse to me several times this week. He has shared it with me "out of the blue," as we call it. He would quote it as we would pass in the hallway, or in the middle of a TV show, or as he would walk into a room I was in. I'm grateful to be reminded of Scripture, whenever it comes!

From Romans 5:3,4, what are three results of trials that strengthen you and draw you closer to Him?

_____

_____

Attitudes Christians should have when going through trials and persecution:

REJOICE: *Rejoice, and be glad, for your reward in heaven is great, for so they persecuted the prophets who were before you. Matthew 5:12*

BE PATIENT: *And we toil, working with our own hands; when we are reviled, we bless; when we are persecuted, we endure. 1 Corinthians 4:12*

GLORIFY GOD: *But if anyone suffers as a Christian, let him not feel ashamed, but in that name let him glorify God. 1 Peter 4:16*

PRAY: *But I say to you, love your enemies, and pray for those who persecute you. Matthew 5:44*

Journal

Use any part of today's reading that encourages you in your trials.

_____

_____

_____

_____

_____

_____

_____

Day 19: Exodus 3:7-8,10-14,20; 4:10-13

And the LORD said, "I have surely seen the affliction of My people who are in Egypt, and have given heed to their cry because of their taskmasters, for I am aware of their sufferings. So I have come down to deliver them from the power of the Egyptians, and to bring them up from that land to a good and spacious land, to a land flowing with milk and honey, to the place of the Canaanite and the Hittite and the Amorite and the Perizzite and the Hivite and the Jebusite.

"Therefore, come now, and I will send you to Pharaoh, so that you may bring My people, the sons of Israel, out of Egypt." But Moses said to God, "Who am I, that I should go to Pharaoh, and that I should bring the sons of Israel out of Egypt?" And He said, "Certainly I will be with you, and this shall be the sign to you that it is I who have sent you: when you have brought the people out of Egypt, you shall worship God at this mountain."

Then Moses said to God, "Behold, I am going to the sons of Israel, and I shall say to them, 'The God of your fathers has sent me to you.' Now they may say to me, 'What is His name?' What shall I say to them?" And God said to Moses, "I AM WHO I AM"; and He said, "Thus you shall say to the sons of Israel, 'I AM has sent me to you.'"

"So I will stretch out My hand, and strike Egypt with all My miracles which I shall do in the midst of it; and after that he will let you go."

Then Moses said to the LORD, "Please, LORD, I have never been eloquent, neither recently nor in time past, nor since Thou hast spoken to Thy servant; for I am slow of speech and slow of tongue." And the LORD said to him, "Who has made man's mouth? Or who makes him dumb or deaf, or seeing or blind? Is it not I, the LORD? Now then go, and I, even I, will be with your mouth, and teach you what you are to say." But he said, "Please, LORD, now send the message by whomever Thou wilt."

After God had revealed to Moses that He was going to deliver His people (Exodus 3:7-8), Moses must have clapped and expressed great joy. That is, until Moses understood God's plan included using Moses. Moses doubted because of his own weakness. But God always provides all that is needed to accomplish His work. Certainly Moses' weakness or Pharaoh's stubbornness could not stand in the way of God's sovereign plan!

The LORD assures Moses with His presence (Exodus 3:12), His character (3:14), and His enabling power (Exodus 3:20). God didn't ask Moses to go and explain all he didn't know about Him. He just asked him to go and explain all he did know. Moses might have said, "I won't have all the answers." God could reply: "You will have all of Me."

Sometimes we are just like Moses. We are slow of tongue but fast with excuses! (Exodus 4:10). It's so easy to see why He should choose someone else. It reminds me of the book, *Here I Am, Send Aaron.* We forget that when God calls us to do something, He gives us His ability and His authority to accomplish it.

Illustration

As I was driving to speak to a women's circle for the first time, I was scared to death. So scared that I pulled my car over in a parking lot one block from the church and asked the Lord to please let me fall and break a leg so I wouldn't have to teach. That was a very dramatic prayer because I hate pain, especially when it's mine!

When I arrived and got out of my car, I was amazed I didn't fall down. What was the Lord thinking? The meeting had already begun (I spent too long begging the Lord to get me out of this), so I sat down on the last row. To make matters worse, my sweet sister had driven eight hours to hear me. She leaned over and asked me two questions. Where had I been and what book of the Bible was I going to teach?

I didn't answer the first question and I couldn't answer the second. I had no idea what I was to teach. Not taking any notes with me that day didn't help matters. They introduced me and as I walked up to the podium with my Bible, I told the Lord I loved Him and asked Him to help me not embarrass Him. Immediately, He brought the lesson back to my memory and replaced my fear with His joy. Times like this allow us to experience the principle: obedience is our outward expression of our love for God.

Journal

What has the LORD highlighted to you through today's reading?

_____

_____

_____

_____

Application

When was the last time you doubted that God would provide everything that was needed to help you accomplish what He asked you to do? What excuses did you make and may still be making to avoid obeying Him? Do you express your love for Him by obeying Him? How will you express your love for Him today? Do you have an obedience problem? If you have an obedience problem, did you know you have a love problem? "If you love Me, you will obey what I command." John 14:15 (NIV)

Principle

Obedience is your outward expression of your love for God.

Day 20: Apply this principle to your life

Obedience is your outward expression of your love for God.

Matthew Henry once said, "God is more glorified and self more denied, by obedience than by sacrifice. It's easier to bring a bullock or lamb to be burned on the altar, than to bring every high thought into obedience to God, and to make our will subject to His will." [4]

> And Samuel said, "Has the LORD as much delight in burnt offerings and sacrifices as in obeying the voice of the LORD? Behold, to obey is better than sacrifice, and to heed than the fat of rams." _I Samuel 15:22_

Obeying the _____ of the _____ is an outward expression of our love for Him. Before we can obey His voice, we first must hear Him. The LORD longs for us to be sensitive to His voice. If you are like me, you are the one usually doing all the talking.

Why is it so hard for us to be silent and listen for His voice as we kneel before His throne?

_____

_____

_____

> And the people said to Joshua, "We will serve the LORD our God and we will obey His voice." _Joshua 24:24_

> For thus the LORD spoke to me with mighty power and instructed me not to walk in the way of this people. _Isaiah 8:11_

> Whether you turn to the right or to the left, your ears will hear a voice behind you, saying, "This is the way; walk in it." _Isaiah 30:21 (NIV)_

Lord, help us be still and quiet long enough to hear your voice. And then, Lord, help us to obey your voice today.

> And this is love, that we walk according to His commandments. This is the commandment, just as you have heard from the beginning, that you should walk in it. _2 John 1:6_

An outward expression of our love is defined as obeying His _____

> And as Jesus passed on from there, He saw a man, called Matthew, sitting in the tax office; and He said to him, "Follow Me!" And he rose, and followed Him. _Matthew 9:9_

In the Greek, "follow" means "to be in the same way with."

We have two dogs. Shadow and Noah. Shadow received his name because he follows you everywhere you go. We inherited Noah from our daughter. Noah's name should be Shadow Junior because he also follows each step you take. I can't tell you how many times I have tripped over them. Something drastically changes when we take them for a walk. They not only won't follow you or your directions, they insist on always being ahead of you. It's become a joke now as we will try and sneak up behind them so we can get in front. They always sense us coming and they dart out ahead.

We're like that sometimes. One day we follow close to our Lord and sometimes we move ahead of Him. My prayer is that we may draw so close to the Lord that we can be seen in His shadow.

Our Lord Jesus Christ is the greatest example of today's principle: obedience is your outward expression of your love for God.

Have this attitude in yourselves which was also in Christ Jesus, who, although He existed in the form of God, did not regard equality with God a thing to be grasped, but emptied Himself, taking the form of a bond-servant, and being made in the likeness of men. And being found in appearance as a man, He humbled Himself by becoming obedient to the point of death, even death on a cross. Philippians 2:5-8

What same attitude should we pray to have today? _____

_____

_____

It's still hard for me to comprehend such a love that would set aside the glory and splendor of heaven in order to come to earth so He could die in our place. Such a God we serve! A God to Whom we can return and express our love by obedience to Him. Oh, Lord, thank You for expressing Yourself to us through Your great love.

Journal

Put your name anywhere in today's Scripture references where there is the personal pronoun, "I" - "we" - "us" - "me" - "you" - "him"

_____

_____

_____

_____

41

Day 21: Malachi 1:1-5; 3:6a,7

*The oracle of the word of the L*ORD *to Israel through Malachi.*

"I have loved you," says the LORD. *But you say, "How hast Thou loved us?" "Was not Esau Jacob's brother?" declares the L*ORD*. "Yet I have loved Jacob; but I have hated Esau, and I have made his mountains a desolation, and appointed his inheritance for the jackals of the wilderness." Though Edom says, "We have been beaten down, but we will return and build up the ruins"; thus says the L*ORD *of hosts, "They may build, but I will tear down; and men will call them the wicked territory, and the people toward whom the L*ORD *is indignant forever." And your eyes will see this and you will say, "The L*ORD *be magnified beyond the border of Israel!"*

"For I, the LORD, **do not change;** *From the days of your fathers you have turned aside from My statutes, and have not kept them. Return to Me, and I will return to you," says the L*ORD *of hosts. "But you say, 'How shall we return?'"*

The Jews who had returned from captivity in Babylon were full of questions. They mainly questioned God's love for them. In essence, they were saying, "We've rebuilt the Temple and the walls around Jerusalem since we returned from captivity, and yet the enemy is still surrounding us. Our crops aren't growing and You said You were coming back. Where are You? Prove Your love to us!" So the LORD sent His prophet Malachi to speak His Word of love. Malachi means "messenger."

God knew His people felt unstable because they were equating His love with their circumstances. What they thought would happen and what was happening were two different things. We equate God's love to our circumstances even today. If we are to have stability in our lives, we must understand the key to Malachi. Everything in life changes except God. "For I the LORD do not change." (Malachi 3:6) That means even His love is unchanging. God's love never changes.

Illustration

My son broke his wrist playing football. I took him to an orthopedic surgeon and as the doctor was telling him how he would have to set his bone before they put a cast on, I began to perspire. He continued explaining the details and I began getting nauseous. Just as he turned around to me to see if I understood the procedure, I was sinking toward the floor. He called for assistance and the next thing I remember was lying on the table with smelling salts under my nose. I glanced over to see my son, and he was fine. (Looking at me a little strangely, but fine.) The doctor said it would be best if I didn't watch anymore and he escorted my son out of the room. After the cast was on, we walked to the car and I put my arm around him and said, "If you ever question my love for you, remember this day. That was love lying on the table."

We all need visual and verbal reminders of love – a memory we can go back to and claim the love we know. Just like the image my son probably still has today of me experiencing his pain because of my great love for him. Whenever you or I question God's love for us, we can always go back to the cross – where He demonstrated and proved His love for us. His love has not changed.

Journal

What has the LORD highlighted to you through today's reading?

_____

_____

_____

_____

_____

_____

_____

_____

_____

_____

_____

_____

_____

_____

Application

Are you questioning God's love for you? If you are, could it be that you might be equating how much God loves you by how happy you are and by what circumstances you're in? Would you confess that to Him right now? You should start by kneeling before the cross, the place He demonstrated and proved His love for you. Do you need stability in your life because the enemy is surrounding you and everything in your life is changing? Make a list of all the things that are changing in your life. Lay it all at His feet and allow Him to work out His best for you in each thing you have listed.

Principle

*God's love
never changes.*

Day 22: Apply this principle to your life
God's love never changes.

May I share some notes I found I had written in my Bible back in 1993? I had gone away for a couple of days to be alone with the Lord and to concentrate on loving Him more. I studied and meditated on the Song of Solomon. Here is a portion of my journal:

"I am amazed that as I studied Your Word and heard You speak, I did not come here to learn to love You more. I'm here to hear You tell me how much You really, truly, truthfully, and tenderly love me."

I want us to look at a few verses and focus on His love for us. This unchanging love that He has for His people is seen in the spiritual marriage we have with Him.

Draw me after you and let us run together! The king has brought me into his chambers. We will rejoice in you and be glad; We will extol your love more than wine. Rightly do they love you. Song of Solomon 1:4

When we are in His chambers, He is _____. When we come out from His chambers, we will _____ in Him, and be _____.

In his shade I took great delight and sat down, and his fruit was sweet to my taste. Song of Solomon 2:3b

He provides us protection from our burdens, so we go and sit down with Him. His fruit is the cross He bore for us because of His great love.

Let his left hand be under my head and his right hand embrace me. Song of Solomon 2:6

His love for us is an incredible, intimate love. May we rest in His arms all day and night.

Listen! My beloved! Behold, he is coming, climbing on the mountains, leaping on the hills! My beloved is like a gazelle or a young stag. Behold, he is standing behind our wall, He is looking through the windows, He is peering through the lattice. Song of Solomon 2:8-9

He is coming! There is nothing that will hold Him back. No mountain is too hard for Him to climb to get to us. Love always finds a way.

My beloved responded and said to me, "Arise, my darling, my beautiful one, and come along. For behold, the winter is past, the rain is over and gone." Song of Solomon 2:10-11

He constantly invites us to come and be with Him. But He gives us a choice. True love never forces itself upon anyone.

Scarcely had I left them when I found him whom my soul loves; I held on to him and would not let him go, until I had brought him to my mother's house, and into the room of her who conceived me. Song of Solomon 3:4

I held onto Him, the lover of my soul. I would not let Him go. I must cling to Him. How I weep that I cannot take you, My beloved, into my mother's house. But how I rejoice knowing she is in heaven. Now, may I take You into my house where my family can witness You in me.

You are altogether beautiful, my darling, and there is no blemish in you.
Song of Solomon 4:7

He sees us, as we will appear. For we will be like Him.

I am my beloved's, and his desire is for me. Song of Solomon 7:10

True eyes have no eyes for "self."

Journal

Personalize any of today's reading.

_____

_____

_____

_____

_____

_____

_____

_____

_____

_____

_____

_____

_____

_____

Day 23: Nehemiah 1:11; 2:1-6,11-12,20

"O LORD, I beseech Thee, may Thine ear be attentive to the prayer of Thy servant and the prayer of Thy servants who delight to revere Thy name, and make Thy servant successful today, and grant him compassion before this man."

Now I was the cupbearer to the king.

And it came about in the month Nisan, in the twentieth year of King Artaxerxes, that wine was before him, and I took up the wine and gave it to the king. Now I had not been sad in his presence. So the king said to me, "Why is your face sad though you are not sick? This is nothing but sadness of heart." Then I was very much afraid. And I said to the king, "Let the king live forever. Why should my face not be sad when the city, the place of my fathers' tombs, lies desolate and its gates have been consumed by fire?" Then the king said to me, "What would you request?" So I prayed to the

God of heaven. And I said to the king, "If it please the king, and if your servant has found favor before you, send me to Judah, to the city of my fathers' tombs, that I may rebuild it." Then the king said to me, the queen sitting beside him, "How long will your journey be, and when will you return?" So it pleased the king to send me, and I gave him a definite time.

So I came to Jerusalem and was there three days. And I arose in the night, I and a few men with me. I did not tell anyone what my God was putting into my mind to do for Jerusalem and there was no animal with me except the animal on which I was riding.

So I answered them and said to them, "The God of heaven will give us success; therefore we His servants will arise and build, but you have no portion, right, or memorial in Jerusalem."

God had forewarned the Israelites that if they continued to disobey, they would one day be captured and taken to a foreign land. At the end of 70 years, God would bring them back to Jerusalem. We read of the returning exiles in the book of Ezra and Nehemiah. As the book of Nehemiah opens, God is giving Nehemiah a burden to travel 800 miles back to Jerusalem to rebuild the walls so his people could once again be protected. For Nehemiah to approach the King of Persia and ask to leave took great courage and confidence. Courage and confidence are two things we need more of today! Confidence comes from believing that God will finish what He starts.

Illustration

A Texan was riding through Tennessee and stopped for gas. "Fill it up," he said as he walked into the station wearing his 10-gallon hat and smoking his big cigar. The Texan walked over to a hillbilly and asked, "Do you live around here?" "That's my farm across the street" he replied. The Texan asked, "How many acres do you have?" Hillbilly answered, "About 80." The Texan said, "Let me tell you about my farm. I can get into my pickup truck early in the morning and start driving in a straight line across my land and by noontime, I will not have come to the end of my property! Now, what do you think about that?" Hillbilly replied, "Yep, I know what you mean. I used to have a pickup truck like that myself!"

Nehemiah had great confidence too, but not worldly self-confidence. He was aware of his own limitations and put no confidence in the flesh. Our confidence should be in God alone: "For the LORD will be your confidence." Proverbs 3:26a

Even though the task ahead would be enormous, Nehemiah went forward with confidence, knowing that it was God Himself Who had called him for this project. "…I did not tell anyone what my God was putting into my mind to do for Jerusalem." (Nehemiah 2:20) In Nehemiah 6:15-16, we see God honored his prayer. "So the wall was completed on the twenty-fifth of the month Elul, in fifty-two days. And it came about when all our enemies heard of it, and all the nations surrounding us saw it, they lost their confidence; for they recognized that this work had been accomplished with the help of our God."

Journal

What has the LORD highlighted to you through today's reading?

_____

_____

_____

_____

_____

_____

_____

_____

Application

What task is God putting on your heart to do? Are you not answering His call because it seems too overwhelming? What are some of your limitations? If it's confidence you are lacking, what should you do? Who does Scripture say will give us success? Read again Nehemiah 2:20a. Shouldn't we be confident that He will bless whatever He begins? "For I am confident of this very thing, that He who began a good work in you will perfect it until the day of Christ Jesus." Philippians 1:6

Principle

Confidence comes from believing that God will finish what He starts.

Day 24: Apply this principle to your life

Confidence comes from believing that
God will finish what He starts.

The LORD will accomplish what concerns me; Thy lovingkindness, O LORD, is everlasting; Do not forsake the works of Thy hands. Psalm 138:8

David expresses confidence in the will of God, not in himself.

Then Hezekiah took the letter from the hand of the messengers and read it, and he went up to the house of the LORD and spread it out before the LORD. Isaiah 37:14

From reading the above verse, what does it tell us we must do before we take the next step?

_____

_____

By placing the matter in God's hands, we are showing Him our limitations and that we put no confidence in the flesh.

By faith even Sarah herself received ability to conceive, even beyond the proper time of life, since she considered Him faithful who had promised.
Hebrews 11:11

Abraham's wife Sarah was 90 years old when the Lord told her she would conceive a child. Yet, she had confidence in God and believed He would do what He had promised.

Nebuchadnezzar took Daniel and others as captives to Babylon. While in exile, Daniel and his three friends refused to bow down to pagan gods. As you read the Scripture below, think about where Daniel's friends' strength and confidence came from in such a fiery trial.

"Now if you are ready, at the moment you hear the sound of the horn, flute, lyre, trigon, psaltery, and bagpipe, and all kinds of music, to fall down and worship the image that I have made, very well. But if you will not worship, you will immediately be cast into the midst of a furnace of blazing fire; and what god is there who can deliver you out of my hands?" Shadrach, Meshach and Abed-nego answered and said to the king, "O Nebuchadnezzar, we do not need to give you an answer concerning this matter. If it be so, our God whom we serve is able to deliver us from the furnace of blazing fire; and He will deliver us out of your hand, O king. But even if He does not, let it be known to you, O king, that

we are not going to serve your gods or worship the golden image that
you have set up."   *Daniel 3:15-18*

From verse 18, what five words could we add to our vocabulary that would
give us confidence in God for our future trials?

_____

Look at one of your hands and repeat each word for each finger, BUT EVEN
IF HE DOESN'T. God may bring someone across your path today that might
need to hear these five words for the fire. Now pray that the Lord would seal
that kind of faith in your heart.

The Lord asked Jeremiah to be His spokesman and because Jeremiah put his
confidence in his own ability, he gave the Lord excuses as to why he should
not. The following Scripture was handed to me by a friend and prayer warrior
as I was walking up to the podium to teach my first Bible study class.

> *"Then I said, 'Alas, Lord GOD! Behold, I do not know how to speak,*
> *because I am a youth.' But the LORD said to me, 'Do not say, "I am a*
> *youth," because everywhere I send you, you shall go, and all that I*
> *command you, you shall speak.' Then the LORD said to me, 'You have seen*
> *well, for I am watching over My word to perform it.'"*   *Jeremiah 1:6-7,12*

As I read these words, I surrendered all my limitations to Him and was able to
speak with His confidence, believing God had called me and He would finish
what He started.

Journal

What from today's reading will help you have an even greater confidence that
God will finish what He started?

_____

_____

_____

_____

_____

_____

_____

_____

_____

Day 25: Acts 12:1-12

Now about that time Herod the king laid hands on some who belonged to the church, in order to mistreat them. And he had James the brother of John put to death with a sword. And when he saw that it pleased the Jews, he proceeded to arrest Peter also. Now it was during the days of Unleavened Bread. And when he had seized him, he put him in prison, delivering him to four squads of soldiers to guard him, intending after the Passover to bring him out before the people. So Peter was kept in the prison, but prayer for him was being made fervently by the church to God. And on the very night when Herod was about to bring him forward, Peter was sleeping between two soldiers, bound with two chains; and guards in front of the door were watching over the prison. And behold, an angel of the Lord suddenly appeared, and a light shone in the cell; and he struck Peter's side and roused him, saying, "Get up quickly." And his chains fell off his hands. And the angel said to him, "Gird yourself and put on your sandals." And he did so. And he said to him, "Wrap your cloak around you and follow me." And he went out and continued to follow, and he did not know that what was being done by the angel was real, but thought he was seeing a vision. And when they had passed the first and second guard, they came to the iron gate that leads into the city, which opened for them by itself; and they went out and went along one street; and immediately the angel departed from him. **And when Peter came to himself, he said, "Now I know for sure that the Lord has sent forth His angel and rescued me from the hand of Herod and from all that the Jewish people were expecting."** *And when he realized this, he went to the house of Mary, the mother of John who was also called Mark, where many were gathered together and were praying.*

King Herod had the apostle James killed by the sword. Then he threw Peter in prison for the third time. Herod put Peter in a maximum-security cell, chained him to two guards and placed another two guards outside his cell. Yet, that didn't stop Peter's family and friends from praying for him. They knew only God had the power and way to free Peter. So they lifted Peter up in fervent prayer.

The word fervent is related to a medical term describing the stretching of a muscle to its limits. Peter's friends were serious about praying for him. We might call it "intensive prayer." We see that God didn't deliver Peter until the last minute. Isn't that just the way God works most of the time? And yet, we find Peter fast asleep right before God releases him from his cell. Because of his faith and trust, he experienced "sound sleep."

Illustration

Most of us have not spent the night chained to a guard in prison, but all of us have had prison experiences. You know what I mean. We are imprisoned in circumstances and chained to our cares: a car that never works…a husband that doesn't work… an illness that brings bedridden blues…a belligerent boss who keeps everyone walking on egg shells.

God can use prison experiences to reveal His power to us. We usually wait until we have been delivered before we choose to acknowledge His power. But what joy it must bring to our Lord when we choose to experience His power while we are having a prison experience! What a joy it must be for Him when we, like Peter, find ourselves enjoying "trusting rest" because His power has given us peace within, even if our circumstances aren't immediately changing.

Journal

What has the LORD highlighted to you through today's reading?

_____

_____

_____

_____

_____

_____

_____

_____

_____

_____

_____

Application

What circumstance is holding you as a prisoner? Do you experience peace because you can trust God with the outcome? How could your present situation be an opportunity for His power to be revealed to you and through you? Who do you know that is fervently praying for you? Who are you fervently praying for? Would you call that person and share Peter's experience?

Principle

Prisons are opportunities for God's power to be revealed.

51

Day 26: Apply this principle to your life

Prisons are opportunities for God's power to be revealed.

At the end of a church meeting, we were asked to pray for the person sitting on our right. I had only met this person one other time, but I will never forget what he said to me — "It's good to pray for one another because I need the prayer and you need the practice." Spiritual and circumstantial prisons are opportunities to give us both practice and prayer. So let's look at both – practicing to rest in the power of God, and praying to be delivered from our prisons.

God can break through any prison by His power and our prayer.

> *I pray that the eyes of your heart may be enlightened, so that you may know what is the hope of His calling, what are the riches of the glory of His inheritance in the saints, and what is the surpassing greatness of His power toward us who believe. These are in accordance with the working of the strength of His might.*   Ephesians 1:18-19

God can break through the prison of loneliness.

> *I WILL NEVER DESERT YOU, NOR WILL I EVER FORSAKE YOU.*   Hebrews 13:5a

> *For my father and my mother have forsaken me, but the LORD will take me up.*   Psalm 27:10

Isaiah 54:5 is a verse especially for those who feel alone because they are a widow, or have been abandoned by their husband, or they are single and desire to have a husband.

> *For your husband is your Maker, whose name is the LORD of hosts; and your Redeemer is the Holy One of Israel, Who is called the God of all the earth.*   Isaiah 54:5

God can break through the prison of worry.

> *Do not keep worrying.*   Luke 12:29 (Now this is a verse to memorize!)

> *Therefore do not be anxious for tomorrow; for tomorrow will care for itself. Each day has enough trouble of its own.*   Matthew 6:34

Take one day at a time. We all have plenty to worry about: school, money, family, job, health, marriage, and children (just to name a few). Certainly the Lord Jesus had more to worry about than we do, but nowhere do we find Him worrying. Worry is a sure sign that we are not in control of a situation that we are trying to control. The more we worry, the more we need to be alone with God. The first thing we should do is to take our worry to Him. Then we need to name it, and ask Him to give His perspective on the situation. Ask Him to forgive you for worrying, because worry is a sin, and then leave the pressure that you are worrying about with Him. He can do far more with it than you can. The next time the enemy tries to bring that same worry up, you can be filled with expectancy and assurance rather than worry. For our God is faithful to hear and answer His children who are in need.

God can break through the prison of anxiety.

Be anxious for nothing, but in everything by prayer and supplication with thanksgiving let your requests be made known to God. And the peace of God, which surpasses all comprehension, shall guard your hearts and your minds in Christ Jesus. Philippians 4:6-7

Casting all your anxiety upon Him, because He cares for you.
1 Peter 5:7

I've never talked with anyone who was anxious about their past. They may be sad, mad, disappointed or happy about it, but not anxious. We are anxious about our future. To overcome anxiety, we must deal with our fear of the future. It may be a deadline you are facing, or a call from the doctor with test results. But whatever it is, the only thing we really need to know is that God is in control. If we truly believe that and know He wants only what is best for us, we will be able to overcome those anxious thoughts we are having.

I have a way of remembering that God is in control. It only takes four fingers. Hold up four of your fingers and say as you look at each one: "God Is In Control." I've done this so much with my family and friends that we don't even have to say anything. We just hold up four fingers to encourage each other. Try it.

Journal

Use any part of today's reading that can help you reduce your level of anxiety.

_____

_____

_____

_____

_____

_____

_____

_____

Day 27: Ephesians 1:1-14

Paul, an apostle of Christ Jesus by the will of God, to the saints who are at Ephesus, and who are faithful in Christ Jesus: Grace to you and peace from God our Father and the Lord Jesus Christ.

Blessed be the God and Father of our Lord Jesus Christ, who has blessed us with every spiritual blessing in the heavenly places in Christ, just as He chose us in Him before the foundation of the world, that we should be holy and blameless before Him. In love He predestined us to adoption as sons through Jesus Christ to Himself, according to the kind intention of His will, to the praise of the glory of His grace, which He freely bestowed on us in the Beloved. In Him we have redemption through His blood, the forgiveness of our trespasses, according to the riches of His grace, which He lavished upon us. In all

wisdom and insight He made known to us the mystery of His will, according to His kind intention which He purposed in Him with a view to an administration suitable to the fullness of the times, that is, the summing up of all things in Christ, things in the heavens and things upon the earth. In Him also we have obtained an inheritance, having been predestined according to His purpose who works all things after the counsel of His will, to the end that we who were the first to hope in Christ should be to the praise of His glory. **In Him, you also, after listening to the message of truth, the gospel of your salvation–having also believed, you were sealed in Him with the Holy Spirit of promise, who is given as a pledge of our inheritance, with a view to the redemption of God's own possession, to the praise of His glory.**

It had been over 30 years since Paul met Jesus on the Damascus road, where in a blinding flash of light, he received forgiveness for his past, a purpose for his present and security for his future. Paul was still awed that God had forgiven him, saved and used him. Even though Paul didn't possess many material belongings, he was secure in all Christ had given him. Here are a few things Paul reminds them about their eternal riches: they are chosen by Him, loved by Him, adopted as His sons and daughters, accepted by Him, redeemed by Him, forgiven by Him, and sealed by Him.

Paul founded the church in Ephesus and ministered there for three years. He wrote this letter to them while under house arrest in Rome. Although his body was securely locked up, his mind and spirit were free in Christ. Security doesn't rest in where we are, but Whose we are. Since prison wasn't off-limits to the risen Christ, He called on Paul to encourage the believers that they were secure because they had all they needed in Christ Jesus. Paul wanted them to know that they were to live like kings because of all they had inherited from Christ

Jesus. They were acting as if they were poor, instead of being awed by their security in Christ.

Illustration

Security was not what we experienced when we came home one night. I entered our home with my three children and discovered that our home had been burglarized. Actually, I thought the burglar was still in the house, so I gathered the children as calmly as I could and told them to come with me next door for a surprise. They love surprises, so they quickly followed me. We called the police and found out the next day that they had caught two men with a bag of our belongings. How would I ever feel secure again? I knew that if I only focused on this one event, I might never experience peace again. Security is much more than believing your house will never be burglarized. Security is knowing and focusing on God's riches we inherit in Christ.

I remember hearing how the Golden Gate Bridge was built in two sections. During its first section of construction, 23 men fell to their deaths into the San Francisco Bay. Before the second section was started, a safety net was built. The work went 25% faster with no loss of life, because the workers had confidence in the security the safety net provided. [5]

We may stumble and fall in life, but knowing we have all we need in Christ Jesus gives us great security.

Journal

What has the LORD highlighted to you through today's reading?

_____

_____

_____

_____

_____

_____

Application

How secure are you in the fact that God has forgiven you and sealed you? Do you realize what spiritual wealth you possess? What is it that you think you must have because it gives you security? Do you want to discover how wealthy you really are? Then add up everything you have that money can't buy, and death can't take away. Then you'll know!

Principle

Security is knowing that you have all you need in Christ Jesus.

Day 28: *Apply this principle to your life*

Security is knowing that you have all you need in Christ Jesus.

How rich do you feel today? Do you live in a big house? Do you drive an expensive car? Do you have a great sum of money in the bank? Do you place your security in these things that will rot, ruin or rust?

How poor do you feel today? Are you still paying for Christmas? Was your husband's salary just cut in half? Are you feeling very insecure because you don't have what your neighbors have? God's riches and the world's riches are different. The world's riches are called material possessions. God's riches are called spiritual blessings; they belong to us, but we must claim them.

I saw a funny cartoon. A lawyer was reading a client's last will and testament to a group of greedy relatives. It read, "I, Bill Jones, being of sound mind and body, spent it all!"

When Jesus wrote His last will and testament for His Church, He made it possible for us to share His riches, His spiritual blessings. He wrote us into His will and wants us to possess all that He has and all that He is. Doesn't it just blow your mind that He calls us His possessions? God's prized possessions are His people. "And they will be Mine," says the LORD of hosts, "on the day that I prepare My own possession, and I will spare them as a man spares his own son who serves him." Malachi 3:17

Let's look at just a few things we possess.

We possess:

Abundant power:

> *Now to Him who is able to do exceeding abundantly beyond all that we ask or think, according to the power that works within us.*
> *Ephesians 3:20*

Abundant life:

> *The thief comes only to steal, and kill, and destroy; I came that they might have life, and might have it abundantly.* *John 10:10*

Abundant grace:

> *And God is able to make all grace abound to you, that always having all sufficiency in everything, you may have an abundance for every good deed.* *2 Corinthians 9:8*

Abundant supplies:

> *And my God shall supply all your needs according to His riches in glory*
> *in Christ Jesus.* Philippians 4:19

Abundant entrance into Heaven:

> *For in this way the entrance into the eternal kingdom of our Lord and*
> *Savior Jesus Christ will be abundantly supplied to you.* 2 Peter 1:11

Hetty Green is the kind of Christian Paul wrote about in Ephesians. She was rich, but she chose to live like a pauper. When Hetty died in 1916, she left an estate valued at over 100 million dollars. She ate cold oatmeal because it cost too much to heat it. Hetty finally had to have her leg amputated because she took so long looking for a free clinic. Hetty wasn't secure. She was so insecure of her future that she couldn't enjoy the present.[6]

Journal

How do you intend to enjoy the present because of all that you possess through Christ?

Day 29: 1 Corinthians 13:1-13

If I speak with the tongues of men and of angels, but do not have love, I have become a noisy gong or a clanging cymbal. And if I have the gift of prophecy, and know all mysteries and all knowledge; and if I have all faith, so as to remove mountains, but do not have love, I am nothing. And if I give all my possessions to feed the poor, and if I deliver my body to be burned, but do not have love, it profits me nothing. Love is patient, love is kind, and is not jealous; love does not brag and is not arrogant, does not act unbecomingly; it does not seek its own, is not provoked, does not take into account a wrong suffered, does not rejoice in unrighteousness, but rejoices with the truth; bears all things, believes all things, hopes all things, endures all things. Love never fails; but if there are gifts of prophecy, they will be done away; if there are tongues, they will cease; if there is knowledge, it will be done away. For we know in part, and we prophesy in part; but when the perfect comes, the partial will be done away. When I was a child, I used to speak as a child, think as a child, reason as a child; when I became a man, I did away with childish things. For now we see in a mirror dimly, but then face to face; now I know in part, but then I shall know fully just as I also have been fully known. **But now abide faith, hope, love, these three; but the greatest of these is love.**

The church at Corinth was exercising their spiritual gifts in the spirit of competition, not love. Paul begins this chapter explaining the value of love, because he knew that if love ruled supreme in their lives, it would correct not only the way they used God's gifts, but it would teach them that without love, nothing would count.

Illustration

One of the dearest things my son-in-law ever said to me was that he never dreamed that he would find someone to love him as much as my daughter loves him. Isn't it the desire of every parent to have a child love and be loved like that?

We can only truly give love when it has first been given to us. And I'm not talking about the kind of love expressed between human beings. It made me think about the day my daughter became a Christian. It is the kind of love God gives us when we belong to Him.

1 John 4:19 says, "We love because He first loved us." And 1 John 4:7 says, "Beloved, let us love one another, for love is from God; and everyone who loves is born of God and knows God."

As you read the following, replace the word "love" with your own name. "Love is patient; love is kind; love is not jealous; love doesn't brag; love is not arrogant; love doesn't act unbecomingly; it does not seek its own; it isn't provoked. Love doesn't keep score when wronged. Love bears all things, believes all things, hopes all things, endures all things; Love never fails." (1 Corinthians 13:4-8) Does that describe you today?

Remember, Jesus loves for the sake of "giving," not "getting." 1 Corinthians 13 love is the kind of love we can give to others, by asking Him to love through us, even when we don't feel like loving. The ability to love like this isn't natural, it's supernatural!

Journal

What has the LORD highlighted to you through today's reading?

_____

_____

_____

_____

_____

_____

_____

_____

_____

_____

_____

_____

Application

Do you realize that nothing we **say** or **give** or **have** or **do** will count if we do not have love? How do you intend to demonstrate your love to your family this week? How could you show love to that difficult person in your life? Would you read again 1 Corinthians 13:4-8, and ask the Lord to show you how to love others in some specific way? Then, would you practice that very way all day today?

Principle

Without love, nothing counts.

Day 30: Apply this principle to your life
Without love, nothing counts.

I was going through some old pictures and keepsakes the other day. Whenever we celebrate one of our grown children's birthdays, we like to put some of their pictures on a board so we can all reflect on how they have changed. I found some pictures they had drawn in pre-kindergarten that had one question, "I love my mom best when..." It must have been for Mother's Day. Here's how they filled in the blank. "I love my mom best <u>when she smiles at me</u>. I love my Mom best <u>when she kisses me</u>. I love my Mom best <u>when she puts on lipstick</u>." Well, I guess I should just be glad they said they loved me! Because without love, nothing counts.

How do you think your grown children, or your husband, or your best friend would answer the following question about you?

I love _____ best when he/she _____
      (your name)

How would you fill in the following about someone special in your life?

I love _____ best when he/she _____
      (their name)

If he/she doesn't live up to your expectations, do you stop loving them?____

Did all your answers reflect active love? _____ Did you love them best when they were doing something for you? _____ Did anyone answer, "I love he/she best when he/she is with me?" or "I love he/she best when I am giving to them?" _____

Let's examine what real love looks like.

Real Love:

Loves the unlovable:

> *So show your love for the alien, for you were aliens in the land of Egypt.*
> *Deuteronomy 10:19*

There may be someone you love that nobody else might love except you and Jesus.

Remains unselfish:

> *Nobody should seek his own good, but the good of others.*
> *1 Corinthians 10:24 (NIV)*

We are all basically very selfish people. What a great opportunity we have to express our love to Him by unselfishly putting others first. Love expects nothing in return, and demands no attention for generosity.

Serves others:

> *He said to him again a second time, "Simon, son of John, do you love Me?" He said to Him, "Yes, Lord; You know that I love You." He said to him, "Shepherd My sheep."* John 21:16

When we love Him, we will make time to serve and shepherd others.

Gives cheerfully:

> *Let each one do just as he has purposed in his heart; not grudgingly or under compulsion; for God loves a cheerful giver.* 2 Corinthians 9:7

Do you give out of desire or duty? _____ A great way to tell if you give out of duty is if you complain about it later.

Christ's love is:

Inseparable:

> *Who shall separate us from the love of Christ? Shall tribulation, or distress, or persecution, or famine, or nakedness, or peril, or sword?* Romans 8:35

Unchangable:

> *Now before the Feast of the Passover, Jesus knowing that His hour had come that He should depart out of this world to the Father, having loved His own who were in the world, He loved them to the end.* John 13:1

Divine:

> *Just as the Father has loved Me, I have also loved you; abide in My love.* John 15:9

Isn't it wonderful to think that the love of Christ is so strong that there is no way He can love you more! And there's no way He can love you any less? And there's no way He can love you any longer than forever? Nothing you can do can change His constant love for you. Accept His acceptance!

Journal

What one thought stood out to you today?

_____

_____

_____

Day 31: 1 Corinthians 11:17-28

But in giving this instruction, I do not praise you, because you come together not for the better but for the worse. For, in the first place, when you come together as a church, I hear that divisions exist among you; and in part, I believe it. For there must also be factions among you, in order that those who are approved may have become evident among you. Therefore when you meet together, it is not to eat the Lord's Supper, for in your eating each one takes his own supper first; and one is hungry and another is drunk. What! Do you not have houses in which to eat and drink? Or do you despise the church of God, and shame those who have nothing? What shall I say to you? Shall I praise you? In this I will not praise you. For I received from the Lord

that which I also delivered to you, that the Lord Jesus in the night in which He was betrayed took bread; and when He had given thanks, He broke it, and said, "This is My body, which is for you; do this in remembrance of Me." In the same way He took the cup also, after supper, saying, "This cup is the new covenant in My blood; do this, as often as you drink it, in remembrance of Me." For as often as you eat this bread and drink the cup, you proclaim the Lord's death until He comes. Therefore whoever eats the bread or drinks the cup of the Lord in an unworthy manner, shall be guilty of the body and the blood of the Lord. **But let a man examine himself, and so let him eat of the bread and drink of the cup.**

Everything Paul taught revolved around 1 Corinthians 13, known as the love chapter. Paul was teaching them here in chapter 11 to examine themselves and come to the Lord's Table with a prepared heart. The Corinthian Christians needed to be reminded that they were to quit fighting over their "rights." Paul didn't see giving up his own rights as a sacrifice. He believed it was a privilege to do something for Jesus, the One Who gave the supreme sacrifice.

Illustration

We used to live in a house with a field in the backyard. One summer, a certain type of tick was carrying an unusual disease. People we knew were becoming ill from it. So I had the health department come out to see if this field where my children played had these particular ticks. The health officials discovered that the field was infested with the ticks, and suggested two things. First, the children shouldn't play in the field, and second, each night the children should examine themselves for ticks before going to bed.

Self-examinations are very important. A proverb in the business world proclaims: the man who takes no inventory finally becomes bankrupt. Sometimes we go through life being religious detectives. We only investigate what others are doing wrong. What we need to do today is to look inward and examine our own motives and hearts. When you see someone act ugly today, will you examine yourself and see if there is anything ugly in you?

A small-town pharmacist overheard a young boy talking on a pay telephone: "Hello, sir, I was calling to see if you need someone to cut your yard. Oh, you already have someone. Well, is he adequate? Oh, he is? Thank you, I was just checking." As the young fellow replaced the receiver, the pharmacist said, "Sorry you didn't get the job." The boy replied, "Oh, no sir. I've got the job. I was just calling to check on myself." [7]

Journal

What has the LORD highlighted to you through today's reading?

_____

_____

_____

_____

_____

_____

_____

_____

_____

_____

_____

_____

_____

_____

_____

Application

Do you spend your day being a religious detective, only investigating what others are doing wrong? When was the last time you examined yourself before the Lord, to see if there is anyone you need to ask forgiveness from or to forgive? Would you pray Psalm 26:2 for yourself today? "Examine me, O LORD, and try me; test my mind and my heart." Is there a particular verse from today's Scripture that you need to apply to your own life?

Principle

Examining yourself before the LORD keeps you humble.

Day 32: Apply this principle to your life

Examining yourself before the LORD keeps you humble.

I had a different kind of examination a few months ago. All I had to do was lay on a table and this machine could see all the way through my bones. When it comes to me examining myself before the Lord, I need help there too.

There are two words we have all probably said over and over. "I can't." "I can't get along with my boss." "I can't give up this affair." "I can't stop overeating." "I can't find time to pray." "I can't forgive him." Actually, these statements are just half-truths, which equal a whole lie. Even if you can't, God says that He will give you His power and strength to help you.

Whenever I have an opportunity to see a book one of my children is reading, I will look to see what they have underlined. My girls are doing a Bible study together now, and as I was looking through one of their study books last week, I found Philippians 4:13 underlined several times. "I can do all things through Christ who strengthens me." We talked about what an important verse that is to really trust. When you put Philippians 4:13 beside one of your "I can't" phrases, those "I can't" phrases just won't hold up. Try it now.

I can't _____

Now add the phrase, "but we can." That means that you and I can become more giving, more loving, and more humble when we allow Him to help us. But first, we need to examine ourselves.

> But examine everything carefully; hold fast to that which is good.
> *1 Thessalonians 5:21*

> Test yourselves to see if you are in the faith; examine yourselves! Or do you not recognize this about yourselves, that Jesus Christ is in you— unless indeed you fail the test?
> *2 Corinthians 13:5*

> Let us examine and probe our ways, and let us return to the LORD.
> *Lamentations 3:40*

> But Thou knowest me, O LORD; Thou seest me; and Thou dost examine my heart's attitude toward Thee.
> *Jeremiah 12:3a*

Once we have been open and honest before the LORD, He can change us and make us more like Him.

Let's look at His humility and then ask Him to help our prideful ways.

Jesus said in Matthew 11:29, "Take My yoke upon you, and learn from Me, for I am gentle and humble in heart; and YOU SHALL FIND REST FOR YOUR SOULS."

He leads the humble in justice, and He teaches the humble His way.
Psalm 25:9

When pride comes, then comes dishonor, but with the humble is wisdom.
Proverbs 11:2

Humble yourselves, therefore, under the mighty hand of God, that He may exalt you at the proper time. *1 Peter 5:6*

Humble yourselves in the presence of the Lord, and He will exalt you.
James 4:10

Why were these believers encouraged to humble themselves?

_____

_____

Is His timing - your timing? _____

Is His timing perfect timing? _____

To sum up, let all be harmonious, sympathetic, brotherly, kindhearted, and humble in spirit. *1 Peter 3:8*

Journal

From any of today's reading, write any thoughts you have about being humble.

_____

_____

_____

_____

_____

_____

_____

_____

_____

_____

_____

_____

_____

Day 33: Philippians 3:7-14

But whatever things were gain to me, those things I have counted as loss for the sake of Christ. More than that, I count all things to be loss in view of the surpassing value of knowing Christ Jesus my Lord, for whom I have suffered the loss of all things, and count them but rubbish in order that I may gain Christ, and may be found in Him, not having a righteousness of my own derived from the Law, but that which is through faith in Christ, the righteousness which comes from God on the basis of faith, that I may know Him, and the power of His resurrection and the fellowship of His sufferings, being conformed to His death; in order that I may attain to the resurrection from the dead. **Not that I have already obtained it, or have already become perfect, but I press on in order that I may lay hold of that for which also I was laid hold of by Christ Jesus. Brethren, I do not regard myself as having laid hold of it yet; but one thing I do: forgetting what lies behind and reaching forward to what lies ahead,** *I press on toward the goal for the prize of the upward call of God in Christ Jesus.*

Paul was about 60 years old when he wrote this letter and had been a follower of Christ for about 30 years. As Paul wrote this book from his prison cell, we wonder how he could speak with such confidence. Is he blind to the four walls that surround him? He speaks as if he is a man of success. How can someone in prison feel successful? One way is by having God's perspective and not the world's. The world's definition of "success" is productivity. Worldly success doesn't necessarily mean that God approves of what you are doing or have done. God's definition of success is faithfulness. "His master said to him, 'Well done, good and faithful slave; you were faithful with a few things, I will put you in charge of many things; enter into the joy of your master.'" Matthew 25:23

And Paul was faithful. Sometimes we get discouraged if our faith is going unrewarded in tangible ways. Paul knew that the best rewards are intangible, permanent and eternal. Here are just a couple of times Paul expressed this:

> *But I am hard-pressed from both directions, having the desire to depart and be with Christ, for that is very much better.*   Philippians 1:23

> *Knowing that from the Lord you will receive the reward of the inheritance. It is the Lord Christ whom you serve.*   Colossians 3:24

Illustration

After teaching a Bible class for 13 years, the class gave me a computer to help me write this book. I had never used a computer before and had many unsuccessful and unproductive days. I would type half a page and it would disappear.

There must be several pages floating up in space because I have yet to find them. God says that success is
not being perfect. Being successful in God's eyes is
when we continue even when we are tired or fearful or
frustrated. Paul understood God's definition of success:
be faithful to Him wherever you are. The disciple John
writes the words of our Lord, "Be faithful until death,
and I will give you the crown of life." Revelation 2:10b

You can get to know someone pretty well by the prayer
request they share with you. I remember a certain friend
every time I read Philippians 3:10: "That I may know
Him, and the power of His resurrection and the fellowship of His sufferings, being conformed to His death."
This prayer warrior gave different prayer requests
weekly for many years, but it seemed to me that her
favorite request was that she would know Him and the
power of His resurrection. I have watched her go
through chemotherapy and I have seen her trust Him in
the hard times as well as the good. Now that's success.
That's faithfulness.

Journal

What has the Lord highlighted to you through today's
reading?

_____

_____

_____

_____

_____

_____

_____

_____

_____

Application

How do you rate yourself in the area of being a "success"? Are you encouraged that even though Paul wasn't perfect, he was a success in God's eyes? Would you ask Him today to help you be faithful to Him, whatever your circumstances might be? When you face pressures today, how can you remember to rejoice rather than complain? What do you need to start counting as rubbish for the sake of Christ?

Principle

*God's definition of success
is faithfulness.*

Day 34: Apply this principle to your life
God's definition of success is faithfulness.

Success is:

Being faithful to ask Him to forgive you.

> *If we confess our sins, He is faithful and righteous to forgive us our sins and to cleanse us from all unrighteousness.*　　　　　*1 John 1:9*

What is the result of confessing your sins? _____

We can rely on His mercy and the righteousness of Christ for free and full forgiveness. That means He has forgiven even all those things you and I did in the past that hurt someone else deeply. He promises us that He has forgiven us "as far as the east is from the west, so far has He removed our transgressions from us." (Psalm 103:12) The Lord said also in Jeremiah 31:34b, "I will forgive their iniquity, and their sin I will remember no more."

How long does He remember our sin? _____

Being faithful to forgive yourself.

I know that it has been much harder for me to forgive myself than for me to forgive others. I was dealing with the pain of an unforgiving spirit against myself not too long ago. The pain within my heart was excruciating. I needed deliverance. I knew that God had promised me that He had forgiven me. That meant I was even being unfaithful to believe that God keeps His promises. Hebrews 10:23 states that very fact: "Let us hold fast the confession of our hope without wavering, for He who promised is faithful."

He Who promised is _____

Therefore there is no question that He will do what He says!

During this time of turmoil within, I began reading the Scriptures on forgiveness over and over. The Lord spoke directly to my heart through Psalm 79:9: "Help us, O God of our salvation, for the glory of Thy name; and deliver us, and forgive our sins, for Thy name's sake." It was the words "for Thy name's sake" that blew me away. I was going against His great name by being unfaithful to forgive myself. His name represents His very character. He is a forgiving God. If God says, "I forgive you," who am I to say, "but I can't forgive myself?" Am I more righteous than God? Are you?

Being faithful to restrain your reactions.

How do you react when you are driving in the right lane and someone pulls over in front of you, gives you a dirty look and honks? Proverbs 19:11 says, "A wise man restrains his anger and overlooks insults. This is to his credit."

Being faithful to master your moods.

Do you live by your commitments, or how you feel at the moment? Proverbs 25:28 says, "Like a city whose walls are broken down is a man who lacks self-control." (NIV)

Watching your words.

Do you speak before you think? Proverbs 13:3 says, "The one who guards his mouth preserves his life; the one who opens wide his lips comes to ruin."

We must remember that God's definition of success is faithfulness. To be a failure, all you have to do is refuse to get up one more time.

It's better to be a follower who fails than one who fails to follow.

Journal

Personalize any of today's reading.

_____

_____

_____

_____

_____

_____

_____

_____

_____

_____

_____

_____

_____

_____

_____

_____

_____

_____

Day 35: Exodus 19:1-6; Deuteronomy 32:9-11

In the third month after the sons of Israel had gone out of the land of Egypt, on that very day they came into the wilderness of Sinai. When they set out from Rephidim, they came to the wilderness of Sinai, and camped in the wilderness; and there Israel camped in front of the mountain. And Moses went up to God, and the LORD called to him from the mountain, saying, "Thus you shall say to the house of Jacob and tell the sons of Israel: 'You yourselves have seen what I did to the Egyptians, and how I bore you on eagles' wings, and brought you to Myself. Now then, if you will indeed obey My voice and keep My covenant, then you shall be My own possession among all the peoples, for all the earth is Mine; and you shall be to Me a kingdom of priests and a holy nation.' These are the words that you shall speak to the sons of Israel."

*For the LORD's portion is His people; Jacob is the allotment of His inheritance. He found him in a desert land, And in the howling waste of a wilderness; He encircled him, He cared for him, He guarded him as the pupil of His eye. **Like an eagle that stirs up its nest, That hovers over its young, He spread His wings and caught them, He carried them on His pinions.***

Exodus 19:1 tells us that it had been three months since God delivered the Israelites from Egypt. Here they are now, 2 to 3 million people camped at the foot of Mount Sinai. Moses gets his people settled and goes up the mountain expecting to meet with God. ("And Moses went up to God..." 19:3a). God met him and told him to be His spokesman. God wanted Moses to speak of His love for them. The first ten words of verse 4 could have given Moses plenty to speak about: "You yourselves have seen what I did to the Egyptians..." Moses could remind them how the LORD had issued the 10 plagues to the Egyptians. He could also reminiscence about the Passover and the passage through the Red Sea. Now that's love. It even looked like love.

In Exodus 19:4b, we think about how in His love He carried them just as an eagle carries her eaglets on her wings. But to see the whole picture of what that verse means, we must go to Deuteronomy 32:9-11. Here we have a better understanding that love doesn't always look like love. God, in His love, stirs up the nest because He knows that sometimes the hard experiences in life draw us closer to Him.

Illustration

When I was in high school, the eagle was our mascot. I thought it was a good choice because an eagle is admired for its strength and ability to soar to great heights. But there is much more to an eagle than that.

An eagle stirs the nest, making the nest uncomfortable by removing some feathers and sticks. The next day the eagle pushes each eaglet out of the nest and swoops down to catch it before it hits the ground. If they weren't prompted, the eaglets would never leave home. The eagle then puts her eaglets on her back and flies around. The eagle wants to teach her young to fly, to grow, and to trust the air currents. Sometimes love doesn't look like love.

I'll never forget driving my two girls to college. We would grab a bite to eat, hit the store and go back to decorate their dorm room. Then came time for me to begin my journey home, alone. There were times I left them on the steps of their dorms crying. Like the eagle, I was helping them learn how to fly on their own. They didn't know it, but I would cry for hours on the way home. Love probably didn't look like love to them then.

Application

How has God been stirring up your nest? Could you recognize His stirring as love even if it doesn't look like love? What has He been removing in your life to help you learn to trust Him more? What do you need to talk to Him about today that you haven't recognized as His love?

Journal

What has the LORD highlighted to you through today's reading?

_____

_____

_____

_____

_____

_____

_____

_____

_____

_____

_____

_____

Principle

Love doesn't always look like love.

Day 36: Apply this principle to your life

Love doesn't always look like love.

Jesus' death didn't always look like love:

> *And they stripped Him, and put a scarlet robe on Him. And after weaving a crown of thorns, they put it on His head, and a reed in His right hand; and they kneeled down before Him and mocked Him, saying, "Hail, King of the Jews!" And they spat on Him, and took the reed and began to beat Him on the head. And after they had mocked Him, they took His robe off and put His garments on Him, and led Him away to crucify Him.*
>
> *Matthew 27:28-31*

Would you agree that this greatest act of love didn't look like love at the time?

_____

> *For God so loved the world, that He gave His only begotten Son, that whoever believes in Him should not perish, but have eternal life.*
>
> *John 3:16*

Who loved you so much that He gave His only Son to die in your place?

_____

Jesus hung on the cross for six hours before He died. But Scripture teaches that His life wasn't taken from Him. He gave it up.

> *For this reason the Father loves Me because I lay down My life that I may take it again. No one has taken it away from Me, but I lay it down on My own initiative. I have authority to lay it down, and I have authority to take it up again. This commandment I received from My Father.*
>
> *John 10:17-18*

Jesus had the _____ to lay His life down.

> *After they have scourged Him, they will kill Him; and the third day He will rise again.*
> *Luke 18:33*

Jesus had the _____ to be raised from the dead.

With all His authority and power, He still chose to give us the gift of eternal life by dying on the cross. He doesn't force His love gift on us. Forced love is not love. Nor does love always look like love.

God's discipline doesn't always look like love:

We need God's discipline because of our sin nature. But as He is disciplining us, we sometimes forget that love doesn't always look like love.

> *For those whom the Lord loves He disciplines.*　　　*Hebrews 12:6*

Whom does the Lord discipline? _____

> *...He disciplines us for our good, that we may share His holiness. All discipline for the moment seems not to be joyful, but sorrowful; yet to those who have been trained by it, afterwards it yields the peaceful fruit of righteousness.*　　　*Hebrews 12:10-11*

He disciplines us for our _____ so we may share in His _____

Discipline may not look like love, but those who have been trained by it will later yield the fruit of peace and _____.

> *And you shall remember all the ways which the LORD your God has led you in the wilderness these forty years, that He might humble you, testing you, to know what was in your heart, whether you would keep His commandments or not. He humbled you and let you be hungry, and fed you with manna which you did not know, nor did your fathers know, that He might make you understand that man does not live by bread alone, but man lives by everything that proceeds out of the mouth of the LORD. Your clothing did not wear out on you, nor did your foot swell these forty years. Thus you are to know in your heart that the LORD your God was disciplining you just as a man disciplines his son.*　　　*Deuteronomy 8:2-5*

God disciplined His people on their journey to teach them important lessons.

Journal

Reflect on the greatest act of love (the crucifixion) that didn't look like love. Then thank Him by naming some of the important lessons the Lord has taught you through discipline.

_____

_____

_____

_____

_____

_____

_____

_____

Day 37: Genesis 2:16-17, 3:1-7

And the LORD **God commanded the man, saying, "From any tree of the garden you may eat freely; but from the tree of the knowledge of good and evil you shall not eat, for in the day that you eat from it you shall surely die."**

Now the serpent was more crafty than any beast of the field which the LORD *God had made. And he said to the woman, "Indeed, has God said, 'You shall not eat from any tree of the garden'?" And the woman said to the serpent, "From the fruit of the trees of the garden we may eat; but from the fruit of the tree which is in the middle of the garden, God has said, 'You shall not eat from it or touch it, lest you die.'" And the serpent said to the woman, "You surely shall not die! For God knows that in the day you eat from it your eyes will be opened, and you will be like God, knowing good and evil." When the woman saw that the tree was good for food, and that it was a delight to the eyes, and that the tree was desirable to make one wise, she took from its fruit and ate; and she gave also to her husband with her, and he ate. Then the eyes of both of them were opened, and they knew that they were naked; and they sewed fig leaves together and made themselves loin coverings.*

Everything was going great in the first home. The garden was perfect. The temperature was perfect. Eve looked over at her husband, and he was perfect! Eve probably possessed the perfect hair and body. There were no worries, burdens, crises, aches, pains, stress, bills or heartaches. It was a perfect day. Then, just like that, Eve was faced with a choice. Looking closely at Genesis 2:16-17, we can see that man's freedom of choice was given when God told them what fruit they could and could not eat.

God wants to be involved in our choices. He didn't make a mechanical man because He wanted a race that would choose to love and obey Him. God cultivates good choices in our lives, while Satan tries to sow bad ones.

Questions such as "where did sin begin?" and "why do we have to die?" come from Genesis 3, which tells the story of man's fall. The serpent (also known as the devil, deceiver, prince of this world, liar and dragon) appeared and tempted Eve. Did you notice how Satan tempted Adam? He didn't. He let Eve tempt him. Satan knows that it's easy for us to be tempted by those who have the most influence on us.

Illustration

I miss the days when my children were little and always around. I remember one hot summer day when my son and his best friend were outside playing. I don't know who influenced whom, but they both came home with a handful of vegetables. They were proud of their gatherings. Their choice seemed good until my neighbor came over to tell me he was not the one who gave the boys the vegetables from his garden. They had made the choice to help themselves. It was probably a great adventure for them to see how much they could acquire without being seen. But they soon discovered that consequences follow choices.

As a teenager, I was invited to go to Florida with one of my friends and her family. Before we left, her mom told me I could do anything I wanted except for one thing: I was not allowed to chew Juicy Fruit gum in the car. I could chew any other kind, but the smell of Juicy Fruit made her nauseous. Our very first stop for gas, we went in to get a drink, and guess what I had to have? You know it – Juicy Fruit gum!

Think about it for a minute. When we are given many choices of things we can have or can do and only one we can't, why do we focus on that one forbidden thing? The choices we are faced with aren't the problem. It's the bad and wrong choices we make that cause us to fall. Satan is always trying to oppose God by tempting us to make bad choices rather than good, godly ones.

Journal

What has the LORD highlighted to you through today's reading?

_____

_____

_____

_____

_____

_____

_____

_____

_____

_____

Application

List some of the choices you are faced with today. If any of your choices go against God's Word, then know you are being tempted by the evil one. What is it you are attracted to that God has forbidden? What will you do today to resist it?

Principle

God wants to be involved in your choices.

75

Day 38: Apply this principle to your life

God wants to be involved in your choices.

Here's some good news/bad news.

"I got married."… "That's good."
"No, that's bad, he's ugly."… "Oh, that's bad."
"No, that's good, he's rich." …"Oh, that's good."
"No, that's bad, he's stingy."… "Oh, that's bad."
"No, he bought me a house." …"Oh, that's good."
"No, that's bad, the house burned."… "Oh, that's bad."
"No, that's good, I didn't like it anyway."

The good news for us today is that our good choices bring God's blessings. The bad news is that our bad choices bring God's judgement or discipline.

Let's look at some good choices we need to make each day.

> *But seek first His kingdom and His righteousness; and all these things shall be added to you.*   *Matthew 6:33*

> *And if it is disagreeable in your sight to serve the LORD, choose for yourselves today whom you will serve: whether the gods which your fathers served which were beyond the River, or the gods of the Amorites in whose land you are living; but as for me and my house, we will serve the LORD.*   *Joshua 24:15*

> *Who is the man who fears the LORD? He will instruct him in the way he should choose.*   *Psalm 25:12*

Even though one may have true faith in the Lord Jesus Christ, he may still have occasions of unbelief. We sometimes question the most important truths. Just another good reason to stay in His Word daily and pray without ceasing.

Adam and Eve did not involve God in their choice. They chose to doubt God rather than believe Him. They made a bad choice. Let's look at some results of our choices.

Results of bad choices:

We experience shame

> *And they heard the sound of the LORD God walking in the garden in the cool of the day, and the man and his wife hid themselves from the presence of the LORD God among the trees of the garden.*   *Genesis 3:8*

I could always tell when my children had done something wrong. They didn't want to be around me. We act the same way when we are guilty before God.

We grieve God

> *How often they rebelled against Him in the wilderness, and grieved Him in the desert!*　　　　　　　　　　　　　　　　*Psalm 78:40*

We stumble and fall

> *For Jerusalem has stumbled, and Judah has fallen, because their speech and their actions are against the* LORD, *to rebel against His glorious presence.*　　　　　　　　　　　　　　　　　*Isaiah 3:8*

Results from good choices:

We experience pleasure and success

> *If they hear and serve Him, they shall end their days in prosperity, and their years in pleasures.*　　　　　　　　　　　　　*Job 36:11*

> *This book of the law shall not depart from your mouth, but you shall meditate on it day and night, so that you may be careful to do according to all that is written in it; for then you will make your way prosperous, and then you will have success.*　　　　　　　　　*Joshua 1:8*

We receive blessing

> *Now therefore, O sons, listen to me, for blessed are they who keep my ways.*　　　　　　　　　　　　　　　　*Proverbs 8:32*

God's blessings are more understood when we go to Matthew 5-7, where our Lord Jesus gave the Sermon on the Mount. Blessed means "happy." The blessings of God bring pleasure and contentment and encouragement to His children. They may come in a physical way and/or material way, but always in the spiritual sense.

The Christian life is full of choices. We need to remember, however, that though the choices are ours, the power is God's.

Journal

Write down the good choices you intend to make today by using any of today's reading. Would you ask the Lord to be involved with any choice you make today?

_____

_____

_____

_____

Day 39: 1 Samuel 30:1-8,17-19

Then it happened when David and his men came to Ziklag on the third day, that the Amalekites had made a raid on the Negev and on Ziklag, and had overthrown Ziklag and burned it with fire; and they took captive the women and all who were in it, both small and great, without killing anyone, and carried them off and went their way. And when David and his men came to the city, behold, it was burned with fire, and their wives and their sons and their daughters had been taken captive. **Then David and the people who were with him lifted their voices and wept until there was no strength in them to weep.** *Now David's two wives had been taken captive, Ahinoam the Jezreelitess and Abigail the widow of Nabal the Carmelite.* **Moreover David was greatly distressed because the people spoke of stoning him, for all the people were embittered, each one because of his sons and his daughters. But David strengthened himself in the LORD his God.**

Then David said to Abiathar the priest, the son of Ahimelech, "Please bring me the ephod." So Abiathar brought the ephod to David. And David inquired of the LORD, saying, "Shall I pursue this band? Shall I overtake them?" And He said to him, "Pursue, for you shall surely overtake them, and you shall surely rescue all."

And David slaughtered them from the twilight until the evening of the next day; and not a man of them escaped, except four hundred young men who rode on camels and fled. So David recovered all that the Amalekites had taken, and rescued his two wives. But nothing of theirs was missing, whether small or great, sons or daughters, spoil or anything that they had taken for themselves; David brought it all back.

After being away from fighting another war, David returned to Ziklag only to find tragedy. His house and the entire city had been burned to the ground. And if that wasn't enough, all the women and children had been kidnapped. And if that wasn't enough, all the men in the city blamed David and wanted to kill him. This tragedy didn't make David the man he was. Tragedies don't make a person. They reveal a person's character. Like his men, David wept, but he didn't look for a scapegoat to blame. Instead, he strengthened himself in the Lord, proving that every problem in life is an opportunity to exercise your faith in God. David could have found strength in the Lord only if he truly believed that God was bigger than this tragedy. David decided to take his eyes off everything else around him and place them on the LORD, Who had guided him, helped him, comforted him and strengthened him so many times before.

Illustration

I've never come home to a burning house or felt someone was out to kill me, but there was a time when I
thought someone had kidnapped my little girl. She was
six years old and I was pregnant with my third child.
We had gone over to my brother's condominium where
his backyard opened onto a golf course. My sister and
her three girls were also visiting from out of town. After all the children had been outside playing for about
an hour, they all came in, except my six-year-old, who
had wandered away. All of us went to search for her.

Like David, I wept. But unlike him, I didn't strengthen
myself in the Lord. To strengthen yourself in the Lord
you must turn to Him, focus on His ability and strength,
and then lean fully on Him. All I did was cry, call for
her, and collapse when I saw her. Someone had found
her walking around on another fairway. She had wandered off and couldn't find her way back.

After we arrived safely home, I felt like I had just exer-
cised every muscle in my body. Looking back, I can
see that the only thing I didn't exercise was my faith in
God.

Journal

What has the LORD highlighted to you through today's
reading?

_____

_____

_____

_____

_____

_____

_____

_____

_____

_____

Application

What was your
last crisis? Did
you look at it as an
opportunity to
exercise your faith
in God? When the
next opportunity
comes, would you
prepare yourself
now to strengthen
yourself in the
Lord rather than
crumble?

Principle

*Every problem in life
is an opportunity to
exercise your faith
in God.*

Day 40: Apply this principle to your life

Every problem in life is an opportunity to exercise your faith in God.

Sometimes we lose an opportunity to exercise our faith in God because:

We fail to pray:

When we look at the story of Jesus taking His disciples to the garden for the last time, we see two different actions: the disciples sleeping and Jesus praying.

> *And He took with Him Peter and the two sons of Zebedee, and began to be grieved and distressed. Then He said to them, "My soul is deeply grieved, to the point of death; remain here and keep watch with Me." And He went a little beyond them, and fell on His face and prayed, saying, "My Father, if it is possible, let this cup pass from Me; yet not as I will, but as Thou wilt." And He came to the disciples and found them sleeping, and said to Peter, "So, you men could not keep watch with Me for one hour? Keep watching and praying, that you may not enter into temptation; the spirit is willing, but the flesh is weak."*   Matthew 26:37-43

Who was exercising their faith in the above verses? _____

Who was not exercising their faith? _____

You can strengthen yourself in the Lord by _____

The battle looks too great:

> *For a wide door for effective service has opened to me, and there are many adversaries.*   1 Corinthians 16:9

When a door of opportunity opens for you, do you not walk through it because there are many adversaries?   Yes   No   Sometimes

Why? _____

_____

We depend on our own strength:

> *Behold, God is my salvation, I will trust and not be afraid; For the LORD GOD is my strength and song, and He has become my salvation.*
>   Isaiah 12:2

> *For Thou hast girded me with strength for battle; Thou hast subdued under me those who rose up against me.*   Psalm 18:39

*For by Thee I can run upon a troop; and by my God I can leap over a
wall.*
                                                              Psalm 18:29

In my Bible, beside Psalm 18:29, I wrote, "Went horseback riding and jumped
for the first time." Whenever I read that verse I am reminded of the following
story.

It was a beautiful November day in 1990 when a friend invited me to go riding
with her. She put me on a horse that was so old, he could barely walk. I think
she just wanted to make sure I didn't get hurt! So we w-a-l-k-e-d for a l-o-n-g
time. I knew her horse was a jumper, so I asked her if I could watch her make
some jumps. I w-a-l-k-e-d my horse back to the barn. Then I went over to the
ring where she was trotting and jumping small jumps. She made it look so easy
and so fun. I begged and she finally consented to let me ride her horse. The
jumps were in the middle of the ring and my horse trotted around the sides.

Now this horse knew what he was doing. I was having so much fun riding and
talking, I wasn't paying any attention to what the horse was about to do. He had
lined himself up to make a jump. By the time I realized what was happening, I
only had two choices. Jump off or hang on. I thought this horse had done this
jump much more than I had (which was never) and knew much more about it
than I did (which was nothing). So, I just dropped the reins and held onto his
mane. Through that experience, I learned to exercise my faith in the horse to do
something I knew nothing about.

Isn't that what God wants us to do with Him? To depend on Him so much that
we will exercise our faith in Him, knowing He knows what He is doing and
exactly how it is to be done. All you and I need to do is drop the reins and cling
to Him.

Finally, be strong in the Lord, and in the strength of His might.
                                                         Ephesians 6:10

Journal

Use any part of today's reading that speaks to a particular situation in your life.

_____

_____

_____

_____

_____

_____

_____

Day 41: 2 Corinthians 10:1-7; Matthew 22:37-38

*Now I, Paul, myself urge you by the meekness and gentleness of Christ— I who am meek when face to face with you, but bold toward you when absent! I ask that when I am present I may not be bold with the confidence with which I propose to be courageous against some, who regard us as if we walked according to the flesh. For though we walk in the flesh, we do not war according to the flesh, for the weapons of our warfare are not of the flesh, but divinely powerful for the destruction of fortresses. **We are destroying speculations and every lofty thing raised up against the knowledge of***

***God, and we are taking every thought captive to the obedience of Christ,** and we are ready to punish all disobedience, whenever your obedience is complete. You are looking at things as they are outwardly. If anyone is confident in himself that he is Christ's, let him consider this again within himself, that just as he is Christ's, so also are we.*

And He said to him, "'You shall love the Lord your God with all your heart, and with all your soul, and with all your mind.' This is the great and foremost commandment."

Paul reminded the Christians in Corinth that there is unseen warfare going on in this world. It's between the force of good (God) and the force of evil (the world, the flesh and Satan). Paul explained in verse 3 that even though they were walking around in the flesh (in human bodies), they were not to fight according to the flesh (human plans and methods) to win their battles. Paul goes on to explain that the weapons needed to fight this war are "divinely powerful" (verse 4). God's weapons – prayer, God's Word and the Holy Spirit – are powerful and effective enough to destroy any stronghold that the world, flesh and Satan might have.

Illustration

We are still in the middle of spiritual warfare today. And we will continue in this war until Christ comes again. Some of the battles we fight against might be alcohol or drugs, anger, bitterness, self-pity or an unforgiving spirit. Satan knows he can't keep a Christian out of heaven, so he attacks you to make you ineffective in your daily walk.

A stronghold occurs when the power of the enemy is holding you down so much that you can't seem to get up to win the battle.

My little girl was six years old when her brother was born. She responded to him as if one of her favorite dolls had come to life. She fed him, rocked him, changed him, carried him on her hip, and played with him. She absolutely loved and adored him. But every once in a while, she would pin him down on the floor so he couldn't move. Nothing he seemed to do could free him from her stronghold.

Say you commit a sin. It's not that big, but over time it becomes a habit. Then it becomes a stronghold in your life. Let's look and see how bitterness can become a stronghold. Someone passes by you and doesn't speak. Instead of thinking that she probably didn't see you, you think that she must be mad at you. If you hold onto that thought, it will grow. Then, the next time you see her, you have already decided you will not speak first and even if she speaks, you just might ignore her. When you entertain a wrong thought, bitterness creeps in and becomes a stronghold in your life.

Two things we need to remember about strongholds. First, we can't free ourselves from them. Second, God can. Only God can break a stronghold. 2 Corinthians 10:5 tells us how. We are to bring every thought into captivity to Jesus. He can free us through His Word and by prayer. We have to know what the Bible says and we have to apply it through prayer.

Did you realize that our greatest battles are won or lost on the threshold of our mind?

Put your hand on your forehead right now as a reminder. The next time a sinful thought comes to your mind, stop right then and ask the Lord to help you stop entertaining that thought so it won't become a stronghold in your life.

Journal

What has the Lord highlighted to you through today's reading?

_____

_____

_____

_____

_____

Application

Write down the definition of a stronghold. What stronghold is there in your life? Are you trying to fight your spiritual battles in the flesh, with your own plans and by your own methods? Who is the only One that can free us from Satan's strongholds? What is your part in winning this battle? Do you need to confess to the Lord your use of a worldly weapon, such as shouting? Slamming? Arguing? Blackmail? Lying? Will you thank Him now for His divine weapons that weaken and destroy Satan's strongholds?

Principle

Only God can break a stronghold.

Day 42: Apply this principle to your life
Only God can break a stronghold.

We have three enemies: the world, the flesh and Satan. Our battle is not against people, but against the system of the world that is trying to control us, the enemy of the flesh that we have inherited, and the spiritual forces of wickedness.

Our battle is not against people, but against the _____, the _____ and _____.

> *I have written to you, fathers, because you know Him who has been from the beginning. I have written to you, young men, because you are strong, and the word of God abides in you, and you have overcome the evil one.*
> *1 John 2:14*

This is the secret of God's great spiritual warriors. The Word of God abides in them. They have saturated themselves with the Word of the Lord. Deuteronomy 17:19 says that we are to read God's Word all the days of our life. Now that's saturating yourself with His Word. It's not enough to have a Bible, or have His Word taught to us. We must study it at home and allow His Spirit to speak to us wherever we are in our walk of life. Max Lucado once said that the Bible is the only book you can sit down with and always have the Author present.

> *Do not love the world, nor the things in the world. If anyone loves the world, the love of the Father is not in him. For all that is in the world, the lust of the flesh and the lust of the eyes and the boastful pride of life, is not from the Father, but is from the world.*   *1 John 2:15-16*

What three things can become a stronghold in our life if we don't bring them to Jesus? _____

_____

_____

The lust of the flesh deals with passions. "I must …"

The lust of the eyes deals with possessions. "I must have…"

The lust of pride deals with position. "I must be…"

Don't get discouraged in this battle. We need to remember victory is ours in Christ Jesus. If there were no opposition, there would be no victory. God can break any stronghold in your life. Then He will become your stronghold. And that's One we don't want to get free from!

The Lord will be our stronghold:

> *The LORD also will be a stronghold for the oppressed, a stronghold in times of trouble.*
> *Psalm 9:9*

The word "stronghold" here means, to protect/a refuge.

> *The LORD is my rock and my fortress and my deliverer, my God, my rock, in Whom I take refuge; my shield and the horn of my salvation, my stronghold.*
> *Psalm 18:2*

> *Because of his strength I will watch for Thee, for God is my stronghold.*
> *Psalm 59:9*

The children called her Mrs. Bible Smith. Her walk with the Lord was one of trust, love and security. God was her stronghold. After she had been diagnosed with cancer, she asked me to pray Psalm103 for her. It is a psalm to praise the Lord for His mercies. In verse three, it speaks of the One who heals all our diseases. The Lord chose to heal her completely by taking her to heaven.

During her final hospital stay, I went and sat by her bed. I asked her one question. "If you could tell me one thing I could do to love the Lord Jesus more, what would it be?" She quoted Matthew 22:37: "You shall love the LORD your God with all your heart, and with all your soul and with all your mind." Every time I read that verse, I think about her and her goal to love Him that much. If you and I would make it our goal today to be aware of loving Him with all of our mind, then we would bring any sinful thought we might have to Him, instead of entertaining them and allowing sin to become a stronghold in our life.

Journal

What do you need to bring to Jesus so it won't become a stronghold in your life (lust of the flesh, lust of the eyes, or pride)?

_____

_____

_____

_____

_____

_____

_____

_____

_____

Day 43: Exodus 1:22; 2:1-10

Then Pharaoh commanded all his people, saying, "Every son who is born you are to cast into the Nile, and every daughter you are to keep alive."

*Now a man from the house of Levi went and married a daughter of Levi. **And the woman conceived and bore a son; and when she saw that he was beautiful, she hid him for three months. But when she could hide him no longer, she got him a wicker basket and covered it over with tar and pitch. Then she put the child into it, and set it among the reeds by the bank of the Nile.** And his sister stood at a distance to find out what would happen to him. Then the daughter of Pharaoh came down to bathe at the Nile, with her maidens walking alongside the Nile; and she saw the basket among the reeds and sent her maid, and she brought it to her.*

When she opened it, she saw the child, and behold, the boy was crying. And she had pity on him and said, "This is one of the Hebrews' children." Then his sister said to Pharaoh's daughter, "Shall I go and call a nurse for you from the Hebrew women, that she may nurse the child for you?" And Pharaoh's daughter said to her, "Go ahead." So the girl went and called the child's mother. Then Pharaoh's daughter said to her, "Take this child away and nurse him for me and I shall give you your wages." So the woman took the child and nursed him. And the child grew, and she brought him to Pharaoh's daughter, and he became her son. And she named him Moses, and said, "Because I drew him out of the water."

Israel was in bondage – slaves to Pharaoh. Pharaoh feared that if the Israelites grew any larger in number, they might turn on him or flee Egypt. So he ordered all male Hebrew babies to be thrown into the Nile. This is when Moses, a Hebrew boy, was born. Yet, we read from Hebrews 11:23 that his parents did not fear the king's command. "By faith Moses, when he was born, was hidden for three months by his parents, because they saw he was a beautiful child; and they were not afraid of the king's edict." Faith in God set them above fearing man. If we do all we know God has called us to do, then we can trust Him with the outcome.

Amram and Jochebed (Moses' parents) believed in the promise God had made to deliver Israel from bondage. Because they were people who put their trust in the character of God, not in what was happening all around them, they hid Moses for the first three months of his life. This was not an easy thing to do with a crying newborn. Maybe this was one of the ways God confirmed to them that He was going to deliver Moses. Maybe there were times when Moses would be crying, a guard would walk by and Moses would immediately stop crying. Eventually, his mom had to act. She put Moses into a basket and set it by the bank of the Nile. She did all she could do and then she trusted God with the outcome. Faith and planning go hand in hand.

Illustration

A friend from out of town came to stay with us. Late one night she shared with me what a hard time she endured with her teenage son. During that difficult year, she was asked to teach from chapter two of Exodus. As tears streamed down her cheeks, she told me what God had taught her as she prepared her lesson. She was to do all she could do for her son and then put him into a basket (figuratively) and watch what God would do. God did a miraculous thing! Her son called home from camp one day and said God had called him into the ministry. It doesn't always work out like it did for my friend or for Moses. But if we do all we know God has called us to do, then we can trust Him with the outcome.

Journal

What has the LORD highlighted to you through today's reading?

_____

_____

_____

_____

_____

_____

_____

_____

_____

_____

_____

Application

What situation or relationship do you need to put in the basket and entrust to God? Do you choose to put your trust in the character of God (His sovereignty, omnipotence, faithfulness, etc.) or in what is happening around you? When you have done all you know God has called you to do, and your situation still looks hopeless, do you give up – or give in by trusting God with it? "So do not fear, for I am with you; do not be dismayed; for I am your God. I will strengthen you and help you; I will uphold you with my righteous right hand." Isaiah 41:10

Principle

Do all God has called you to do, then trust Him with the outcome.

Day 44: Apply this principle to your life

Do all God has called you to do,
then trust Him with the outcome.

There are some expressions we use. "I'm in a pickle." "I'm up a creek without a paddle." "I'm between a rock and a hard place." These expressions all describe a situation in which you can't see the way out. Have you ever been there?

Let's look at a situation the Israelites experienced: they did all God had told them to do and then they trusted Him with the outcome.

The Lord had heard the cries of His people who were enslaved in Egypt and sent Moses to set His people free. Pharaoh finally agreed to let His people go after God had sent the 10 plagues. This is where we will pick up the story.

> *Now it came about when Pharaoh had let the people go, that God did not lead them by the way of the land of the Philistines, even though it was near; for God said, "Lest the people change their minds when they see war, and they return to Egypt." Hence God led the people around by the way of the wilderness to the Red Sea; and the sons of Israel went up in martial array from the land of Egypt.* Exodus 13:17-18

_____ led the people to the _____

Notice here that the Israelites did what God had called them to do. They left Egypt.

> *Now the LORD spoke to Moses, saying, "Tell the sons of Israel to turn back and camp before Pi-hahiroth, between Migdol and the sea; you shall camp in front of Baal-zephon, opposite it, by the sea. For Pharaoh will say of the sons of Israel, 'They are wandering aimlessly in the land; the wilderness has shut them in.' Thus I will harden Pharaoh's heart, and he will chase after them; and I will be honored through Pharaoh and all his army, and the Egyptians will know that I am the LORD. And they did so."* Exodus 14:1-4

What did the LORD say Pharaoh would do? _____

_____

What would Pharaoh and all his army and the Egyptians learn from this situation?

> *Then the Egyptians chased after them with all the horses and chariots of Pharaoh, his horsemen and his army, and they overtook them camping by the sea, beside Pi-hahiroth, in front of Baal-zephon. And as Pharaoh*

drew near, the sons of Israel looked, and behold, the Egyptians were marching after them, and they became very frightened; so the sons of Israel cried out to the LORD.

Exodus 14:9-10

The Israelites saw the clouds of dust from the approaching Egyptian army.

So they cried out to _____

But Moses said to the people, "Do not fear! Stand by and see the salvation of the LORD which He will accomplish for you today; for the Egyptians whom you have seen today, you will never see them again forever."   *Exodus 14:13*

Can't you just hear the people? "Sure, Moses, fear not. The mountains are on one side of us, the sea is behind us and the Egyptian army is in front of us!"

When God has you backed up to the sea and there's nothing else you can do, stand firm and don't fear. Get excited about how God will deliver you. Don't get in His way. Imagine what would have happened that day if the Israelites had decided to fight Pharaoh's army by the sea? Again, here's the principle: do all God has called you to do, stand firm and trust Him with the outcome.

You know the end of the story. God told Moses to lift up his staff and stretch his hand over the sea. Moses did what God called him to do, and then God did the rest. The sea was divided, the Israelites crossed over to safety and Pharaoh's army drowned.

Journal

Personalize Exodus 14:9-10. What are you crying out to the LORD about today because of fear? What will help that fear according to Exodus 14:13?

_____
_____
_____
_____
_____
_____
_____
_____
_____

Day 45: 1 Thessalonians 1:1-9

Paul and Silvanus and Timothy to the church of the Thessalonians in God the Father and the Lord Jesus Christ: Grace to you and peace.

We give thanks to God always for all of you, making mention of you in our prayers; **constantly bearing in mind your work of faith and labor of love and steadfastness of hope in our Lord Jesus Christ in the presence of our God and Father,** *knowing, brethren beloved by God, His choice of you; for our gospel did not come to you in word only, but also in power and in the Holy Spirit and with full conviction; just as you know what kind of men we proved to*

be among you for your sake. You also became imitators of us and of the Lord, having received the word in much tribulation with the joy of the Holy Spirit, so that you became an example to all the believers in Macedonia and in Achaia. For the word of the Lord has sounded forth from you, not only in Macedonia and Achaia, but also in every place your faith toward God has gone forth, so that we have no need to say anything. For they themselves report about us what kind of a reception we had with you, and how you turned to God from idols to serve a living and true God...

The apostle Paul wrote to a group of new believers who were facing extreme pressures. His purpose in writing was to comfort, strengthen, and encourage them. Just hearing Paul tell them how he thanked God for their spiritual growth (verses 1-4) must have helped them tremendously. Paul had recognized their work as a work of faith and a labor of love. He sounds like a proud father. And indeed he was. When Paul had previously been there, he had preached Christ to these people who practiced a pagan religion. Could verse 1:9 be the secret to labor out of love rather than out of obligation? Work isn't labor when it's a labor of love. The God they served now was a living God, not a lifeless idol. He was a true God, not a false god.

Illustration

Have you ever been faced with extreme pressures? Have you ever had a really bad day? Do you know how to tell it is going to be one? Here are a few signs. You call 911 and they put you on hold! You can't find your glasses and they are already on your face. Your boss tells you not to bother to take off your coat! You put both contact lenses in the same eye! What do you do when your day starts off badly and gets worse? How do you face pressures? When they come, does that make you serve the Lord out of obligation rather than out of love?

So often we forget that serving the Lord is a privilege. Sometimes we serve as if we are being forced to do something we don't want to do. The story of the millionaire from Texas makes this point. A Texan gave a barbecue for over 100 people. He gathered everyone near the pool and threw a chicken tied to string into the water. When he pulled the string out, nothing but bones was left. The pool was full of piranhas. The wealthy Texan said, "Whoever will swim the length of this pool can have either 10,000 acres with cattle, or 12 oil wells or my daughter's hand in marriage." All of a sudden they heard the water splash and a guy jumped out of the pool. When asked what he wanted, he replied, "I want 5 minutes with the guy who pushed me in."

May we not feel or act like we labor for Christ because we were pushed into it. May we labor with love because of all He has done, is doing and will do for us!

A little girl was carrying a big baby. A man passed by and asked, "Isn't that baby too heavy for you?" "Oh no," said the little girl, "he's my brother." Work isn't labor when it's a labor of love.

Journal

What has the LORD highlighted to you through today's reading?

_____

_____

_____

_____

_____

_____

_____

_____

_____

Application

Who is that someone in your life who is thankful for your spiritual growth? If he/she were sitting there beside you now, what would you want to say to him/her? Why not call or write that special person and thank them personally? How do you think others observe your work, as a labor of love or obligation? Whether it is in your home or workplace, where do you need to adjust your attitude and work out of love rather than obligation?

Principle

Work isn't labor when it's a labor of love.

Day 46: Apply this principle to your life

Work isn't labor when it's a labor of love.

How Jesus saw His work:

> *Jesus said to them, "My food is to do the will of Him who sent Me, and to accomplish His work."* John 4:34

Jesus saw His work as nourishing and energizing as _____

> *For I have come down from heaven, not to do My own will, but the will of Him who sent Me.* John 6:38

Jesus came to do whose will? _____

How we are to see and do our work:

> *For we are His workmanship, created in Christ Jesus for good works, which God prepared beforehand, that we should walk in them.*
> Ephesians 2:10

Believers in Christ Jesus were created for _____

> *All Scripture is inspired by God and profitable for teaching, for reproof, for correction, for training in righteousness; that the man of God may be adequate, equipped for every good work.* 2 Timothy 3:16-17

> *Let your light shine before men in such a way that they may see your good works, and glorify your Father who is in heaven.* Matthew 5:16

When others see Him shining through our good works it brings _____ to the Father. Knowing that should help our work be a labor of love.

> *For we are God's fellow workers; you are God's field, God's building.*
> I Corinthians 3:9

Who is working with us? _____ We are never working alone.

> *Whatever you do, do your work heartily, as for the Lord rather than for men.* Colossians 3:23

How are you to do your work? _____ You are to do your work as working for _____, not for men.

That means when you are cleaning out the refrigerator because your husband asked, or you are typing a report for your boss on your day off, you can remember you are doing it as for the Lord.

> *Thus says the LORD, "Restrain your voice from weeping, and your eyes*

from tears; for your work shall be rewarded," declares the LORD.
Jeremiah 31:16

For God is not unjust so as to forget your work and the love which you have shown toward His name, in having ministered and in still ministering to the saints.
Hebrews 6:10
(Write your own name in place of "your" and "you")

Your work will be _____ and will not be _____ by the Father.

Does that mean He will only reward missionaries and forget all the business workers and housewives who demonstrate His love to others? If you answered yes, please go back and read again the two verses above.

If anyone serves Me let him follow Me; and where I am, there shall My servant also be; if anyone serves Me, the Father will honor him.
John 12:26

According to John 12:26, why should I do my best even when no one is looking?

_____

Not only will the Father honor you, but He is always with you. He sees all that you do. He was even with Noah when he was on the ark. And nowhere do we hear of Noah complaining about his work. Not even shoveling manure for all those animals. Our work may not always be pleasant or uplifting—just ask Noah! Our work doesn't have to be labor when it's a labor of love.

Journal

Make a plan as to how you intend to work within your home or in the office, using today's Scripture verses.

_____

_____

_____

_____

_____

_____

_____

_____

_____

93

Day 47: John 11:1-10,14-15,40

Now a certain man was sick, Lazarus of Bethany, the village of Mary and her sister Martha. And it was the Mary who anointed the Lord with ointment, and wiped His feet with her hair, whose brother Lazarus was sick. The sisters therefore sent to Him, saying, "Lord, behold, he whom You love is sick." **But when Jesus heard it, He said, "This sickness is not unto death, but for the glory of God, that the Son of God may be glorified by it."** *Now Jesus loved Martha, and her sister, and Lazarus. When therefore He heard that he was sick, He stayed then two days longer in the place where He was. Then after this He said to the disciples, "Let us go to Judea again." The disciples said to Him, "Rabbi, the Jews were just now seeking to stone You, and are You going there again?" Jesus answered, "Are there not twelve hours in the day? If anyone walks in the day, he does not stumble, because he sees the light of this world. But if anyone walks in the night, he stumbles, because the light is not in him."*

Then Jesus therefore said to them plainly, "Lazarus is dead, and I am glad for your sakes that I was not there, so that you may believe; but let us go to him."

Jesus said to her, "Did I not say to you, if you believe, you will see the glory of God?"

Lazarus was sick and his two sisters sought Jesus for help. Verse three doesn't even use Lazarus' name: ("he whom You love is sick.") They must have thought that He would surely jump at the chance to heal such a close friend. After all, Jesus, the great physician, had healed many strangers. It doesn't take much imagination to see what was happening. Mary and Martha knew where Jesus was when they sent for Him. They probably took turns sitting with Lazarus so one could wait for Jesus to arrive. You probably would have heard them ask people who passed by if they had seen Him coming. They waited. They prayed. They watched their brother die.

Jesus loved Lazarus, Mary and Martha. Yet, He made no appearance for two whole days. Then (verses 7 and 8), Jesus tells His disciples it is time to go to Bethany. But they tried to stop Him for fear He might get stoned. Jesus' eye was on the timing of God, not man's timing. Jesus could have said at this point, "Boys, it could be worse. After this we are going to Jerusalem and they are going to crucify Me."

Illustration

We have one of our greatest struggles between the time we ask the Lord for help and the time He moves and helps us. That L-O-N-G time between the "Help!" and the "Happening." Maybe you are there now. You've cried out to Him for help and all you hear is an echo of your cry. Could it be He is waiting to do something even greater in order to reveal His power and His love and His glory? Raising Lazarus from the dead revealed even greater power and love and glory than healing his sickness. God never brings about a situation that cannot bring Him glory.

My spiritual mentor went to the doctor and discovered she had some cells that looked suspicious. She had a biopsy and cancerous cells were removed. When I called to see how she was doing, she replied, "If I have cancer and God wants to use my cancer for His glory, then it's alright with me." See why she is my spiritual mentor? I heard her teach God's Word for years and I knew that her response to this situation was indicative of her life's aims. First, that God be glorified. Second, that He would use her to bring others to Himself. She knew that God never puts you in a situation in which you cannot bring Him glory.

Sometimes we can see what God is up to. Sometimes we can't. One thing we do know. God is in the business of glorifying Himself and bringing others to know Him.

Journal

What has the LORD highlighted to you through today's reading?

_____

_____

_____

_____

_____

_____

_____

_____

_____

Application

Are you in that L-o-n-g time between the "Help!" and the "Happening?" What are you asking Him to help you with and what is happening? Would you acknowledge today that He might have you waiting in that place so He can reveal something even greater in your life? After you acknowledge that, would you then record what you expect Him to do based on today's reading?

Principle

God never puts you in a situation in which you cannot bring Him glory.

Day 48: Apply this principle to your life

God never puts you in a situation
in which you cannot bring Him glory.

Now to the King eternal, immortal, invisible, the only God, be honor and glory forever and ever. Amen. 1 Timothy 1:17

Pleasing God brings Him glory:

"And He who sent Me is with Me; He has not left Me alone, for I always do the things that are pleasing to Him." John 8:29

What did Jesus always do? _____

Since we are to be like Jesus, what should we always strive to do? _____

_____

Therefore also we have as our ambition, whether at home or absent, to be pleasing to Him. 2 Corinthians 5:9

Children, be obedient to your parents in all things, for this is well-pleasing to the Lord. Colossians 3:20

But just as we have been approved by God to be entrusted with the gospel, so we speak, not as pleasing men but God, who examines our hearts. 1 Thessalonians 2:4

Fruitfulness brings Him glory:

By this is My Father glorified, that you bear much fruit, and so prove to be My disciples. John 15:8

When we _____ we bring Him glory. John 15 says we can only bear much fruit if we abide/cling to Him.

Suffering as a Christian brings Him glory:

But if anyone suffers as a Christian, let him not feel ashamed, but in that name let him glorify God. 1 Peter 4:16

Let's look at the life of Joseph and continue applying the principle: God never puts you in a situation in which you cannot bring Him glory.

Twenty-five percent of the book of Genesis is about the story of Joseph, the son of Jacob, who was thrown in the pit by his own brothers, sold as a slave as a teenager and taken to Egypt. Genesis 37 begins the story that doesn't end until chapter 50. It reads as a suspense novel that tells of a hero being dumped on way too long. The theme of Genesis runs throughout Joseph's story. Although God made everything good and man's sin spoiled it, God has not given up. We can trust Him and we can always bring Him glory in our situations.

Even though Joseph had been rejected and hated by some of his own family members, listen to what he says to them when he sees them 22 years later. The scene is one where the brothers now fear for their lives because of all they had done to Joseph. "But Joseph said to them, 'Do not be afraid, for am I in God's place? And as for you, you meant evil against me, but God meant it for good in order to bring about this present result, to preserve many people alive.'" Genesis 50:19-20

Joseph had become the Prime Minister of Egypt and saved millions of people from starvation, even his own family. Joseph is a model of grace for us. He led by grace, spoke by grace, forgave by grace, forgot by grace and loved by grace. We need to emulate this model by surrendering our hard place to Him and allowing God to use it however He wants and for as long as is needed for our good and for His glory.

Journal

Use today's Scriptures to determine how you will bring Him glory from your circumstances today.

_____

_____

_____

_____

_____

_____

_____

_____

_____

_____

_____

_____

_____

_____

Day 49: James 1:1-6,12-17

James, a bond-servant of God and of the Lord Jesus Christ, to the twelve tribes who are dispersed abroad, greetings.

Consider it all joy, my brethren, when you encounter various trials, knowing that the testing of your faith produces endurance. **And let endurance have its perfect result, that you may be perfect and complete, lacking in nothing.**

But if any of you lacks wisdom, let him ask of God, who gives to all men generously and without reproach, and it will be given to him. But let him ask in faith without any doubting, for the one who doubts is like the surf of the sea driven and tossed by the wind.

Blessed is a man who perseveres under trial; for once he has been approved, he will receive the crown of life, which the Lord has promised to those who love Him. Let no one say when he is tempted, "I am being tempted by God"; for God cannot be tempted by evil, and He Himself does not tempt anyone. But each one is tempted when he is carried away and enticed by his own lust. Then when lust has conceived, it gives birth to sin; and when sin is accomplished, it brings forth death. Do not be deceived, my beloved brethren. Every good thing bestowed and every perfect gift is from above, coming down from the Father of lights, with whom there is no variation, or shifting shadow.

Most commentaries agree that James, the brother of our Lord Jesus, wrote this book. James wrote to these believers because they were having problems living out the life they professed to believe. The first verse tells us that many were scattered because they were under great persecution. They became discouraged because of all the trials and, like us, they needed to be reminded that there is a great difference between trials and temptations.

Trials are used by God to build us up and make us mature. Temptations are used by Satan to tear us down and make us miserable. Satan deals in fear – God deals in faith. Satan wants to make us stumble – God wants to make us stand.

Illustration

I'll never forget the day my oldest daughter came to me and asked the dreaded question – "Mom, when can I start dating?" My reply was: "When you are mature." Guess what her next question was: "What is maturity?" Well, I didn't even have to pray about that! When you hear my answer you will know it was not a spiritual answer. "Darling, you are mature when you eat steak with mushrooms and listen to classical music." "Well, Mom, may I have a steak with mushrooms on top for dinner tonight and listen with you?"

James' definition of maturity was more of what God is aiming for in our lives. This chapter in James is telling us that God uses the trials in our lives to make us *spiritually mature.*

Someone asked a great sculptor one day, "If you had a rock and you wanted to sculpt a horse, what's the first thing you would do?" His response was: "I'd knock off everything that didn't look like a horse." That's what God is doing in my life and yours. He continues to chisel off anything that doesn't look like Jesus. The more we look and act like Him, the more mature we become.

Journal

What has the LORD highlighted to you through today's reading?

_____

_____

_____

_____

_____

_____

_____

_____

_____

_____

_____

_____

_____

Application

Are you having problems living out the life you profess to believe? What trial are you going through that you can choose to see as an instrument God is using to mature you? Is that instrument your husband, your boss, your wayward child, or that car of yours that won't start? Will you thank Him for loving you so much that He will not leave you as you are, an unfinished work, but will continue sculpting away until you are complete in Him?

Principle

God uses trials to make us mature, not miserable.

Day 50: Apply this principle to your life

God uses trials to make us mature, not miserable.

No matter what age you are passing through – the young, middle, or "my, you're looking good" age – God is striving to mature you. Spiritual maturing doesn't have anything to do with age. It has to do with looking like Him and walking in His ways.

> *Whoever claims to live in Him must walk as Jesus did.*
>
> *1 John 2:6 (NIV)*

James 1:2 says trials will come. It doesn't say they may come. So you and I can expect them. Then, when they come, we can remember that He wants to use them for our good.

According to James 1:1-17, a mature person is:

1:1 A serving person	1:9-10 A humble person
1:2 A joyful person	1:12 A persevering person
1:5 A wise person	1:13-15 An overcomer
1:6 A praying person	1:17 A grateful person
1:8 A stable person	

A mature person hungers for God's Word:

> *Like newborn babes, long for the pure milk of the word, that by it you may grow in respect to salvation.*
> *1 Peter 2:2*

> *For ground that drinks the rain which often falls upon it and brings forth vegetation useful to those for whose sake it is also tilled, receives a blessing from God.*
> *Hebrews 6:7*

May we be so thirsty for Him that we will be like the dry ground that drinks in the rain!

Do you read His Word more this year than last year? _____

A mature person listens to God:

> *Concerning Him we have much to say, and it is hard to explain, since you have become dull of hearing.*
> *Hebrews 5:11*

> *Many therefore of His disciples, when they heard this said, "This is a difficult statement; who can listen to it?"*
> *John 6:60*

> *Be still, and know that I am God.*
> *Psalm 46:10a (NIV)*

I have a plaque of Psalm 46:10 sitting on my desk. It reminds me every day that I need to listen more to God. I have a hard time listening. Here are four obstacles to listening. (These will apply not only to how we listen to God, but also to how we listen to other people.)

1. Talking too much. How can we receive information when we are always sending? **Be a receiver.**

2. Being preoccupied. How can we truly listen while we think about something else? **Be an attentive friend.**

3. Being impatient. How can we practice patience, even when a person speaks slowly? **Be a patient person.**

4. Not concentrating. How can we focus on what the person is saying? **Be a focused friend.**

Ask a friend today to tell you what kind of listener you are. Then practice the four keys to listening well.

Journal

What areas do you need the most help from our LORD to be more spiritually mature?

_____

_____

_____

Day 51: Ephesians 6:10-24

*Finally, be strong in the Lord, and in the strength of His might. Put on the full armor of God, that you may be able to stand firm against the schemes of the devil. **For our struggle is not against flesh and blood, but against the rulers, against the powers, against the world forces of this darkness, against the spiritual forces of wickedness in the heavenly places.** Therefore, take up the full armor of God, that you may be able to resist in the evil day, and having done everything, to stand firm. **Stand firm therefore,** HAVING GIRDED YOUR LOINS WITH TRUTH, **and** HAVING PUT ON THE BREASTPLATE OF RIGHTEOUSNESS, and having shod YOUR FEET WITH THE PREPARATION OF THE GOSPEL OF PEACE; in addition to all, taking up the shield of faith with which you will be able to extinguish all the flaming missiles of the evil one. And take THE HELMET OF SALVATION, and the sword of the Spirit, which is the word of God. With all prayer and petition pray at all times in the Spirit, and with this in view, be on the alert with all perseverance and petition for all the saints, and pray on my behalf, that utterance may be given to me in the opening of my mouth, to make known with boldness the mystery of the gospel, for which I am an ambassador in chains; that in proclaiming it I may speak boldly, as I ought to speak.*

But that you also may know about my circumstances, how I am doing, Tychicus, the beloved brother and faithful minister in the Lord, will make everything known to you. And I have sent him to you for this very purpose, so that you may know about us, and that he may comfort your hearts.

Peace be to the brethren, and love with faith, from God the Father and the Lord Jesus Christ. Grace be with all those who love our Lord Jesus Christ with a love incorruptible.

When Paul wrote this letter, he was chained to a Roman guard. Maybe from observing these soldiers, he gives us the picture of the armor we are to put on in order to stand against the schemes of the devil. We need to put on all seven pieces of armor so that we leave no area unguarded. One piece, the belt, can apply to Ephesians 6:14. The belt holds everything together. God's truth is like that belt. It holds everything together in our lives. Satan wants you to doubt God's goodness, love, grace, and compassion. He knows that once a lie gets into the life of a believer, everything else begins to fall apart.

The existence of Satan is taught in seven books in the Old Testament, and all twenty seven books in the New Testament. He is called a murderer, accuser, liar, and tempter. He tries to hinder the believer's work for Christ. Paul said in 1 Thessalonians 2:18, "For we wanted to come to you–I, Paul, more than once–and yet Satan thwarted us."

When we feel the battle is too great, we need to remember that when Lucifer (Satan) fell, only ⅓ of the angels went with him, leaving ⅔ on our side. Satan is powerful, but the LORD is all-powerful. Satan is mighty, but the LORD is almighty. Revelation 20:10 tells us that Satan and his demons have limited time left.

2 Thessalonians 2:8 tells us that the day will come when the Lord Jesus will slay them with the breath of His mouth. How wonderful! Until that day, stand firm. Our belief determines our actions. The Greek word for "stand" means to hold our ground. Our task is to hold the ground Christ has already won for us in His victory at Calvary.

Our highest joys come in our greatest victories, and our finest victories come from our most bitter battles.

Illustration

Putting our two girls to bed at night was a long process. From rides on our backs to baths and stories, the light was finally turned off. That is, until one of them yelled that there was a witch in the closet! Repeatedly responding to their cries, we would go back in and open the closet door, showing them that there was no witch.

Have you noticed that when we believe something, we will act on that belief? Just as their actions showed they feared the witch in the closet, we too will act on what we believe.

Journal

What has the LORD highlighted to you through today's reading?

_____

_____

_____

_____

_____

_____

_____

Application

In spiritual battles, what area are you being attacked in the most? Have you been listening to the father of lies? Can you see Satan hindering your work for Christ? As you put on your clothes today, will you put on the whole armor of God? Since the belt of truth holds everything together, will you determine to stay in His Word and stand on His words? Will you act on the truth that "Greater is He that is in you, than he that is in the world"? 1 John 4:4

Principle

Our beliefs determine our actions.

Day 52: Apply this principle to your life
Our beliefs determine our actions.

When I was growing up, a bully lived down the street from me. He would throw darts at people. He never threw one at me, but he would at my girlfriend. I remember the day he threw one so hard that it stuck in the back of her leg. We had learned not to play near his house, but one day he came where we were and began to bully her. A crowd gathered quickly to see what she would do. She was shaking in her boots and so was I. The next thing we knew, her father stepped from the crowd and stood beside his daughter. It was amazing to watch her relax and become very brave. It's easier to stand when you know someone is standing with you and for you.

Isn't that true in our spiritual walk? It's easier to stand against the devil when you know God is standing with you.

Let's look at three different people whose beliefs determined their actions.

Enoch enjoyed God's presence and walked with Him:

Enoch walked with God for 300 years. Genesis 5 tells us that he didn't start walking with God until he was 65 years old. You only spend that much time walking with someone if you have a whole lot to share. Enoch made time to be with God because he enjoyed being with Him.

How long have you been walking with God? _____

Do you enjoy spending time with Him? _____

Why do you think it is worth your time to walk with Him? _____

_____

What will you do today to make time to be with Him? _____

_____

Enoch enjoyed God's presence and walked with Him. Enoch's belief determined his behavior.

Abraham believed in God's timing and followed Him:

Genesis 12 tells us that Abraham obeyed God and left the comfort of his home and the fellowship of his friends to go to an unseen, unknown destination. To others it must have seemed insane. How could he do it? Abraham believed in God's timing and so he obeyed. Abraham's focus wasn't on the tents or the desert or the sand. Hebrews 11:10 says he was looking for the city with foundations, whose architect and builder is God.

When God says to go, do you go immediately? _____

When God says to wait, how long do you wait? _____

Do you believe that God's timing is perfect? _____

Rahab believed God was dependable in impossible situations and trusted Him:

Joshua 2 tells us that Rahab was a prostitute living in Jericho who concealed Joshua's spies because she believed God was with Joshua. She believed that this same God would save her from her impossible situation. So she trusted Him with her very life and Hebrews 11:31 tells us she did not perish.

Do you believe that you can depend on God when you are in what looks like an impossible situation? _____

Why do you think you can? _____

_____

_____

Remember that your beliefs determine your actions.

Journal

How do your actions reveal what you think about God?

_____

_____

_____

_____

_____

_____

_____

_____

_____

_____

_____

_____

_____

Day 53: 2 Samuel 5:10-11; 1 Chronicles 22:3-5; 1 Kings 8:17-19

And David became greater and greater, for the LORD God of hosts was with him.

Then Hiram king of Tyre sent messengers to David with cedar trees and carpenters and stonemasons; and they built a house for David.

And David prepared large quantities of iron to make the nails for the doors of the gates and for the clamps, and more bronze than could be weighed; and timbers of cedar logs beyond number, for the Sidonians and Tyrians brought large quantities of cedar timber to David. And David said, "My son Solomon is young and inexperienced, and the house *that is to be built for the LORD shall be exceedingly magnificent, famous and glorious throughout all lands. Therefore now I will make preparation for it." So David made ample preparations before his death.*

"Now it was in the heart of my father David to build a house for the name of the LORD, the God of Israel. But the LORD said to my father David, 'Because it was in your heart to build a house for My name, you did well that it was in your heart. Nevertheless you shall not build the house, but your son who shall be born to you, he shall build the house for My name.'"

David was enjoying a period of peace in Jerusalem. Yet, David was deeply troubled. While he was living in a house of cedar, the ark (representing God's presence) was residing in a tent. "Now David built houses for himself in the city of David; and he prepared a place for the ark of God, and pitched a tent for it." 1 Chronicles 15:1

From the time Moses led the Israelites out of Egypt, they had worshipped God in a tented tabernacle. David desired to build a temple – a permanent house for God – not just a tent. David's desire was great, but God said "No." God had other plans. God's plan was for David's son, Solomon, to construct His temple.

Illustration

From a very early age, I have tried to phrase questions in such a way so the answer would not be an adamant "NO." I guess we don't really like to be told "No" until we are spiritually mature enough to know that when God says "No" to something we ask, it is so He may say "Yes" to something better. Accepting God's "No" requires as great a faith as carrying out His "Yes." Do you believe that? Sometimes we do; sometimes we don't.

David accepted God's "NO" by submitting to God's will. David teaches us how we are to respond when God says "No." If we read 1 Kings 8:12-55, we discover that even though David knew he wouldn't be the one to build the temple for God, he still risked his life gathering materials that his son, Solomon, would need to construct the temple. Even though God gave David's dream to Solomon…He allowed David to help in its fulfillment.

George Mueller, a man of great faith, said, "I seek to get my heart into such a state that it has no will of its own."

Journal

What has the LORD highlighted to you through today's reading?

_____

_____

_____

_____

_____

_____

_____

_____

_____

_____

_____

_____

_____

_____

_____

_____

_____

_____

Application

Have you ever thought of something great you wanted to do for God and He said "No"? How did you handle God's "No"? Did you murmur, or accept it by submitting to His will? How strong is your will today? Do you need to get your heart into such a state that it has no will of its own?

Principle

Accepting God's "No" requires as great a faith as carrying out His "Yes."

Day 54: Apply this principle to your life
Accepting God's "No" requires as great a faith as carrying out His "Yes."

The LORD's knowledge and wisdom is so much greater than ours. Why do we ever think that He is wrong to tell us "No" about something we have asked? We are foolish when we try to make His plans and purposes conform to ours. Our goal must be to strive to fit into His plans.

I had asked the LORD for years to allow me to do a particular thing for Him that would have given me great pleasure. That door never opened. I was heartbroken until I discovered 1 Kings 8:18. "But the LORD said to my father David, 'Because it was in your heart to build a house for My name, you did well that it was in your heart.'" I knew God had heard my desire and would even bless me for having the desire, but He had chosen someone else to do that particular thing for Him and had chosen something else for me. It is times like this I go to His Word and claim that His ways are different from mine.

God's ways are higher than man's:

> *"For My thoughts are not your thoughts, neither are your ways My ways," declares the LORD. "For as the heavens are higher than the earth, so are My ways higher than your ways, and My thoughts than your thoughts."* Isaiah 55:8-9

How much higher are the heavens than the earth? _____

This is one blank that will be blank until we get Home. We can't even comprehend the answer.

God's ways are always right:

> *Whoever is wise, let him understand these things; whoever is discerning, let him know them. For the ways of the LORD are right, and the righteous will walk in them, but transgressors will stumble in them.* Hosea 14:9

How many times have you been "right" this week? _____

That doesn't even compare with His average of 100% of always being right.

God's ways are always just:

> *"Now I, Nebuchadnezzar, praise, exalt, and honor the King of heaven, for all His works are true and His ways just, and He is able to humble those who walk in pride."* Daniel 4:37

God's ways are always true:

> *And they sang the song of Moses the bond-servant of God and the song of the Lamb, saying, "Great and marvelous are Thy works, O Lord God, the Almighty; Righteous and true are Thy ways, Thou King of the nations."*
> *Revelation 15:3*

God's ways are unfathomable:

> *Oh, the depth of the riches both of the wisdom and knowledge of God! How unsearchable are His judgments and unfathomable His ways!*
> *Romans 11:33*

From the list above, write the five ways of God that are different from our ways: _____

_____

_____

_____

_____

Journal

What one thing are you asking the LORD to let you do or have but you believe He is saying "No"? What Scripture from today's reading will help you to accept His "No"?

_____

_____

_____

_____

_____

_____

_____

_____

_____

_____

_____

_____

Day 55: Acts 8:26-36

*But an angel of the Lord spoke to Philip saying, "Arise and go south to the road that descends from Jerusalem to Gaza." (This is a desert road.) And he arose and went; and behold, there was an Ethiopian eunuch, a court official of Candace, queen of the Ethiopians, who was in charge of all her treasure; and he had come to Jerusalem to worship. And he was returning and sitting in his chariot, and was reading the prophet Isaiah. And the Spirit said to Philip, "Go up and join this chariot." **And when Philip had run up, he heard him reading Isaiah the prophet, and said, "Do you understand what you are reading?"** And he said, "Well, how could I, unless someone guides me?" And he invited Philip to come up and sit with him. Now the passage of Scripture which he was reading was this:*

"HE WAS LED AS A SHEEP TO SLAUGHTER; AND AS A LAMB BEFORE ITS SHEARER IS SILENT, SO HE DOES NOT OPEN HIS MOUTH. IN HUMILIATION HIS JUDGMENT WAS TAKEN AWAY; WHO SHALL RELATE HIS GENERATION? FOR HIS LIFE IS REMOVED FROM THE EARTH."

And the eunuch answered Philip and said, "Please tell me, of whom does the prophet say this? Of himself, or of someone else?" And Philip opened his mouth, and beginning from this Scripture he preached Jesus to him. And as they went along the road they came to some water; and the eunuch said, "Look! Water! What prevents me from being baptized?"

Philip was told by an angel of the LORD to go to Gaza, which is a desert road that wasn't used very often. The LORD knew that there would be a man from Ethiopia on that same road, seeking to know more about Him. From Acts 8:26, we learn that God communicated His thoughts to us. He told Philip where to go and even when to leave. What if Philip had delayed going? But Philip did obey the voice of the LORD, and his obedience brought growth. His obedience brought spiritual growth to the seeking heart of the Ethiopian and Philip's walk with the LORD.

This Ethiopian eunuch was the secretary to the Queen's treasurer. He had great wealth and a very important position. Yet, there was something missing in his life...so much so that he traveled over 1,000 miles to come to Jerusalem to worship God. Even though he had come to worship God, we learn that he didn't have a personal relationship with the Lord Jesus.

When Philip arrived on the scene, the Ethiopian was reading a passage from Isaiah 53, which gives a clear prediction of the suffering Messiah. Acts 8:35 records that Philip preached Jesus to him. The LORD cared enough about him to send Philip to help him understand this passage he was reading. Philip met him right where he was and helped him to understand.

Illustration

I needed help and I didn't even realize what was happening. God kept sending people like Philip into my life to help me understand God's Word. Unlike the Ethiopian, I was saved, but I was not growing because I wasn't studying His Word and applying it to my own life. I couldn't count the invitations I turned down to go to a Bible study that could have helped me understand how to look more like Jesus and less like Fran. Needless to say, my priorities were way out of whack. There is a verse that describes me from the age of 12 (when I was saved) to the age of 30, when I finally started feeding on God's Word. 1 Corinthians 3:2 says, "I gave you milk to drink, not solid food; for you were not yet able to receive it. Indeed, even now you are not yet able." I couldn't receive the meat of His Word because I was like a baby who has to be fed only milk. Growth comes from reading and applying God's Word to your life.

I thank Him for all the years He sent me invitations through many people. I truly regret all the years I wasted – the peace, joy, love, forgiveness, guidance, assurance, and meaning to life that already belonged to me as His child.

Journal

What has the LORD highlighted to you through today's reading?

_____

_____

_____

_____

_____

_____

_____

_____

_____

Application

Who has the Lord sent to help you understand His Word? How many invitations have you turned down to go to a Bible study? What are your priorities that keep you from studying and appropriating His Word? What areas of growth have you seen in your own life since you have been obedient to Him by studying His Word through this devotional?

Principle

Growth comes from reading and applying God's Word to your own life.

Day 56: *Apply this principle to your life*

Growth comes from reading and applying God's Word to your own life.

When one of my son's friends went off to seminary, I claimed the following verse for him: "Thy words were found and I ate them, and Thy words became for me a joy and the delight of my heart; for I have been called by Thy name, O LORD God of hosts." (Jeremiah 15:16) In fact, I have prayed this verse for my family and me for many years. For I have learned that food for the inner man is the Word of God.

If we would devour God's Word, it would become a _____ and the _____ of our hearts. It's not the facts in our head but truth in our hearts that makes us grow in the Lord. Do you seek the Lord or just read the Bible? _____

God's Word is food for the soul:

And He humbled you and let you be hungry, and fed you with manna which you did not know, nor did your fathers know, that He might make you understand that man does not live by bread alone, but man lives by everything that proceeds out of the mouth of the LORD. Deuteronomy 8:3

God's Word is divinely inspired and written for our instruction:

All Scripture is inspired by God and profitable for teaching, for reproof, for correction, for training in righteousness. 2 Timothy 3:16

For whatever was written in earlier times was written for our instruction, that through perseverance and the encouragement of the Scriptures we might have hope. Romans 15:4

God's Word produces faith:

So faith comes from hearing, and hearing by the word of Christ. Romans 10:17

Psalm 119 refers to God's Word in 171 verses out of its 176. It conveys the thought that the Word of God contains everything man needs to know. The Psalmist uses 10 different terms for the Word of God: the law, instruction, revelation, testimonies, precepts, ways, statutes, decrees, commandments, and ordinances.

There are many benefits from studying the Word of God. Let's look at 7 benefits from Psalm 119:

That we may not sin.

Thy word I have treasured in my heart, that I may not sin against Thee.
Psalm 119:11

Strengthens us.

My soul weeps because of grief; strengthen me according to Thy Word.
Psalm 119:28

Guides us.

Thy word is a lamp to my feet, and a light to my path.   *Psalm 119:105*

Brings us joy.

I have inherited Thy testimonies forever, for they are the joy of my heart.
Psalm 119:111

Gives us understanding.

The unfolding of Thy words gives light; it gives understanding to the simple.   *Psalm 119:130*

Gives us peace.

Those who love Thy law have great peace. And nothing causes them to stumble.   *Psalm 119:165*

Helps us to remember God.

I have gone astray like a lost sheep; seek Thy servant, for I do not forget Thy commandments.   *Psalm 119:176*

Journal

What benefits do you desire to receive the most today from studying God's Word?

_____

_____

_____

_____

_____

_____

_____

_____

_____

_____

_____

Day 57: Psalm 51:1-7,10,16-17

For the choir director: A Psalm of David, when Nathan the prophet came to him, after he had gone in to Bathsheba.

Be gracious to me, O God, according to Thy lovingkindness; According to the greatness of Thy compassion blot out my transgressions. Wash me thoroughly from my iniquity, And cleanse me from my sin. For I know my transgressions, And my sin is ever before me. **Against Thee, Thee only, I have sinned, And done what is evil in Thy sight, So that Thou art justified when Thou dost speak, And blameless when Thou dost judge.**

Behold, I was brought forth in iniquity, And in sin my mother conceived me. Behold, Thou dost desire truth in the innermost being, And in the hidden part Thou wilt make me know wisdom.

Purify me with hyssop, and I shall be clean; Wash me, and I shall be whiter than snow.

Create in me a clean heart, O God, And renew a steadfast spirit within me.

For Thou dost not delight in sacrifice, otherwise I would give it; Thou art not pleased with burnt offering. The sacrifices of God are a broken spirit; A broken and a contrite heart, O God, Thou wilt not despise.

In 2 Samuel, we see that even King David had the potential to fall into sin. After he committed adultery with Bathsheba, he began to lie to cover it up. When lying wasn't enough to cover his sin, he had Bathsheba's husband murdered. The more we try to cover up a sin, the more insensitive we become toward it. I believe most talk shows today reveal the insensitivity of sin. Instead of being ashamed, talk show guests are proud to let the world know their sinful actions.

David tried to go on with his life as if nothing had happened. But he became physically sick. Hear what David was really going through during that time: "When I kept silent about my sin, my body wasted away through my groaning all day long. For day and night, Thy hand was heavy upon me; my vitality was drained away with the fever heat of summer." (Psalm 32:3-4). We learn from David's experience that sin can spread and sicken our lives, if it goes unchecked and unconfessed.

Illustration

My daughter called me one day from school in tears. She was in the first grade and had gone outside with her class to eat lunch. She wasn't hungry, so she threw her lunch sack in the bushes. Her guilt of littering made her miserable, so she called me to talk about it. She was one of those children who couldn't cover up sin for very long. She reminds us all of a very important principle: sin is easier to confess when it first occurs.

Maybe as a child, you had that sick feeling guilt can give. Guilt can make us miserable if we don't face it and acknowledge it as our friend. When we see guilt as our warning signal, we can use four steps from Psalm 51 to confess our sin:

1. Address God (51:1-2)
2. Admit the sin (51:3-5)
3. Acknowledge our part (51:16-17)
4. Ask for forgiveness (51:6-7,10)

We need to approach God with a willingness to obey, a sensitivity to hear, a desire to be cleansed and an attitude of deep respect that He alone deserves.

Journal

What has the LORD highlighted to you through today's reading?

_____

_____

_____

_____

_____

_____

_____

_____

_____

_____

_____

_____

Application

How do you respond when you know you have committed a sin? Do you acknowledge your guilt as a friend, or do you just allow it to make you miserable? Would you pray and ask the Holy Spirit to magnify your sins – those you cannot or will not see? Then will you bring your sin to His throne of grace and address God, admit the sin, acknowledge your part and ask for forgiveness?

Principle

Sin is easier to confess when it first occurs.

Day 58: *Apply this principle to your life*

Sin is easier to confess when it first occurs.

As an adult, do you look back over your life and feel like you missed out on something? I did. That is until I went to a class for 12 weeks on "Adult Children of Alcoholics." It seemed like everyone in that class had one thing in common. We all had a great desire to be "whole" because we came from an "unwholesome" past. Yet, the baggage we were still carrying seemed to be weighing us down enough that we just couldn't seem to get there. What the LORD taught me through that study was that I couldn't change the past or any person – except myself. And if I wanted to be "whole," I could. I was just trying to get there the wrong way.

Guess how we can be whole no matter where we come from or what we've done in the past? Well here's a hint. The word "holy" is derived from the same root word of the English word "whole." Holiness means wholeness. Holiness means being complete. Most of us want to be whole, but not holy. Can't do it. We can't be whole without being holy!

Holiness/Wholeness means:

- Growing in the character of God.
- Being set apart.
- Having an undivided heart.
- Having a single focus.

Holiness/wholeness increases when we become more sensitive to our sins because we are more aware of His heart.

God's heart is full of holiness:

Jesus put tremendous emphasis on holiness. He was holy and His heart's desire is for us to be holy.

> Because it is written, "YOU SHALL BE HOLY, FOR I AM HOLY."
>
> *1 Peter 1:16*

Holiness begins with God, not man. It is when we see His holiness and His hatred for sin that we begin to grasp that our sin is against Him only.

God's heart is full of compassion, graciousness, patience, lovingkindness and truth:

> Then the LORD passed by in front of him and proclaimed, "The LORD, the LORD God, compassionate and gracious, slow to anger, and abounding in lovingkindness and truth."
>
> *Exodus 34:6*

There is none like Him:

> *For this reason Thou art great, O Lord God; for there is none like Thee,*
> *and there is no God besides Thee, according to all that we have heard*
> *with our ears.*   *2 Samuel 7:22*

Holiness means being fully devoted and dedicated to God. The more we grow in holiness – the very character of God – the more we will hate sin.

Our sin reveals God's hatred of sin:

For it was our sin that killed His Son. How can we stand neutral toward that which caused God's Son to suffer and die? Unless we learn to detest sin, we'll never be able to cultivate holiness/wholeness. Sin is anything that doesn't look like God.

In A.D. 59, Paul said that he was the least worthy of all the apostles. (1 Corinthians 15:9) Five years later, Paul said he was less than the least of all God's people. (Ephesians 3:8 NIV) One year after that, Paul stated that he was the greatest sinner of all. (1 Timothy 1:15)

The longer Paul walked with the LORD, the more sensitive he became to sin in his life. Not because he sinned more, but because he saw more.

Do you feel more or less sinful than you did a year ago? _____

Journal

From today's reading how can you be more sensitive to your sins by becoming more aware of His heart?

_____

_____

_____

_____

_____

_____

_____

_____

_____

_____

_____

117

Day 59: Hebrews 11:1-8,23-27

Now faith is the assurance of things hoped for, the conviction of things not seen. *For by it the men of old gained approval. By faith we understand that the worlds were prepared by the word of God, so that what is seen was not made out of things which are visible. By faith Abel offered to God a better sacrifice than Cain, through which he obtained the testimony that he was righteous, God testifying about his gifts, and through faith, though he is dead, he still speaks. By faith Enoch was taken up so that he should not see death; AND HE WAS NOT FOUND BECAUSE GOD TOOK HIM UP; for he obtained the witness that before his being taken up he was pleasing to God. And without faith it is impossible to please Him, for he who comes to God must believe that He is, and that He is a rewarder of those who seek Him. By faith Noah, being warned by God about things not yet seen, in reverence prepared an ark for the salvation of his* household, by which he condemned the world, and became an heir of the righteousness which is according to faith. By faith Abraham, when he was called, obeyed by going out to a place which he was to receive for an inheritance; and he went out, not knowing where he was going.

By faith Moses, when he was born, was hidden for three months by his parents, because they saw he was a beautiful child; and they were not afraid of the king's edict. By faith Moses, when he had grown up, refused to be called the son of Pharaoh's daughter; choosing rather to endure ill-treatment with the people of God, than to enjoy the passing pleasures of sin; considering the reproach of Christ greater riches than the treasures of Egypt; for he was looking to the reward. By faith he left Egypt, not fearing the wrath of the king; for he endured, as seeing Him who is unseen.

Everyone has faith. There are different ways people express faith. The main difference is the object of that faith. Today we might be placing all our faith in the stock market, insurance policies, our spouse or another person. The Hebrew Christians were still putting their faith in the things they could see and touch – like their ritual temple and sacrifices. The writer of Hebrews reminds them that instead of misplacing faith in things, faith needs to be grounded in the right person. His name is Jesus.

Faith is believing everything God says is true and basing every outcome in your life on His Word. Faith does not just believe that a man can walk on a tight rope over Niagara Falls while pushing a wheelbarrow with you inside; real faith is getting in and letting him push you across.

Illustration

While walking up a mountain, a man lost his footing and fell over a cliff. As he fell, he grabbed a branch that was growing from the side of the cliff. Realizing he could not hang on much longer, he called for help.

He cried: "Is there anybody up there?"
A Voice answered: "Yes, I'm here."
He asked: "Who are you?"
The Voice replied: "The Lord."
He pleaded: "Lord, please help me!"
The Lord asked: "Do you trust Me?"
He said: "I trust you completely."
God said: "Good, let go of that branch...I said, let go of that branch."
After a long pause the man yelled, "Is there anybody else up there?"[8]

Journal

What has the LORD highlighted to you through today's reading?

_____

_____

_____

_____

_____

_____

_____

_____

_____

_____

_____

Application

Where are you placing your faith today? Do you know Him well enough to hold fast to what He says is true, even if the world is telling you something different? Would you place your faith in Him today to guide your steps? Do you have to see something to believe it, or can you trust that God is working in your situation even if you can't see a change yet? From the Scripture today, whom would you most want to resemble? Abel? Enoch? Noah? Abraham? Or Moses? Why?

Principle

Faith is believing what God says is true.

Day 60: Apply this principle to your life

Faith is believing what God says is true.

Sometimes people don't like to walk with me because I will shut my eyes and depend on them to lead me. I've done that since I was a little girl. I like to see who I can trust and who I can't. Sometimes they tell me that I can trust them, but they lead me off the path.

Isn't it wonderful to know that everything God says is true? Maybe one of the following verses might be what you need to hang onto in your life today. Be sure and pray the first verse for yourself before you go on to read the others.

> And the apostles said to the Lord, "Increase our faith!"   *Luke 17:5*

What situation today calls you to have more faith? _____

_____

_____

> I have been crucified with Christ; and it is no longer I who live, but
> Christ lives in me; and the life which I now live in the flesh I live by faith
> in the Son of God, who loved me, and delivered Himself up for me.
> *Galatians 2:20*

This verse was Paul's philosophy of life. He gave up the right to run his own life when he gave his life to Christ. When we admit we can't run our lives, He will.

Do you have enough faith today to ask Him and allow Him to run your life?

_____

I mean all of your decisions you need to make, all the ways you are to respond, all your emotions, and your very time schedule? _____

> It was for freedom that Christ set us free; therefore keep standing firm
> and do not be subject again to a yoke of slavery.   *Galatians 5:1*

I have a name plaque someone gave me with my name and its meaning. Frances means "freedom." It is taken from the above Scripture, Galatians 5:1. I love to think that I am free. What am I free to do? Again we must go back to Galatians 2:20. Then we know, like Paul, Christ set us free to live for Him and allow Him to live His life through us. We are free with our new nature to die to hurt feelings, die to cutting remarks, die to gossip, die to our temper, and basically die to our flesh. We can't live this Christian life. But He can through us. We are free to live by faith in a God Who will never fail us.

For we walk by faith, not by sight. *2 Corinthians 5:7*

Do you have to see to believe? _____

How exciting is that? Try this great adventure: verbalize a specific situation to Him, surrender it totally to Him, trust Him with it, and then WATCH for Him to act. Now that's living!

I would have despaired unless I had believed that I would see the goodness of the LORD in the land of the living. *Psalm 27:13*

Sometimes life is so hard that the only thing that keeps us going is our faith and the belief that all suffering will end and we will arrive to our destination – a heavenly home.

Strengthening the souls of the disciples, encouraging them to continue in the faith, and saying, "through many tribulations we must enter the kingdom of God." *Acts 14:22*

We need to encourage each other to _____ in the faith.

Journal

How do you want Him to live through you today? Look at your schedule for today so you can be so specific in the situation requiring faith, that you won't miss when God acts. Live by adventurous faith.

_____

_____

_____

_____

_____

_____

_____

_____

_____

_____

_____

_____

Day 61: Ephesians 3:17-20; 4:1-3; 5:1

...so that Christ may dwell in your hearts through faith; and that you, being rooted and grounded in love, may be able to comprehend with all the saints what is the breadth and length and height and depth, and to know the love of Christ which surpasses knowledge, that you may be filled up to all the fullness of God.

Now to Him who is able to do exceeding abundantly beyond all that we ask or think, according to the power that works within us,

I, therefore, the prisoner of the Lord, entreat you to walk in a manner worthy of the calling with which you have been called, *with all humility and gentleness, with patience, showing forbearance to one another in love, being diligent to preserve the unity of the Spirit in the bond of peace.*

Therefore be imitators of God, as beloved children.

Paul compares the Christian life to walking because it starts with…a step of faith…involves progress…and demands strength. In chapters 4 and 5, Paul gives the believer many practical things he should do to experience a "worthy walk." But Paul, knowing believers would need help to be humble, gentle, patient, loving and truthful, gives the secret for a worthy walk in Ephesians 3:20: "Now to Him who is able to do exceeding abundantly beyond all that we ask or think, according to the power that works within us." This means that the Christian walk isn't based on our own outward efforts, but on God's mighty inward working. Isn't that great news?

In Ephesians 5:1, we are reminded that we are to be imitators of Him. That tells us right away that our first responsibility is to ask Him to reveal those areas of our lives that don't look like Him, then confess it, and trust Him to help us correct that part of our walk. For we are called to be Christ's representatives here on earth.

Illustration

I read of a reverend who spoke at the funeral of his friend. He referred to the dates on her tombstone from the beginning…to the end. He noted that first came the date of her birth, and spoke of the following date with tears, but he reflected that what mattered most of all was the DASH between those years:

> "For that DASH represents all the time she spent living on the earth, and now only those who loved her know what that little line is worth. For it matters not, how much we own; the cars, the house, the cash. What matters most is how we live and love, and how we spend our DASH. So think about this long and hard, are there things you'd like to

change? For you never know how much time is left. You could be at DASH mid-range.

If we could just slow down long enough to consider what is true and real, and always try to understand the way that people feel. And be less quick to anger and show appreciation more. And love the people in our lives like we've never loved before. If we treat each other with respect, and more often wear a smile, remembering that this special DASH might only last a little while.

So when your eulogy is being read with your life's actions to rehash...would you be pleased with the things they say about how you spent your DASH?" [9]

Journal

What has the LORD highlighted to you through today's reading?

_____

_____

_____

_____

_____

_____

_____

_____

_____

_____

_____

_____

Application

Is your "dash" being spent for yourself or for God? When loved ones look at the "dash" in your life, what do you want them to remember about you? More importantly, what do you want to do today that will begin to make your "dash" look like gold so it will be pleasing to the Father?

Principle

God enables us to live our DASH walking worthy of His calling.

Day 62: Apply this principle to your life

God enables us to live our DASH
walking worthy of His calling.

Reminder: Our "dash" represents all the time we spend on this earth. Knowing we are to spend our life worthy of His calling, how can we? Well, we can't. Not in our own power, anyway. Our walking depends on His working.

You are filled right now with something. You may be full of envy, unforgiveness, pride or hatred. Or, you may be filled with contentment, a forgiving spirit, humility or love. As you read the following prayer of Paul, think about what fills you.

> *And I pray that you, being rooted and established in love, may have power, together with all the saints, to grasp how wide and long and high and deep is the love of Christ, and to know this love that surpasses knowledge—that you may be filled to the measure of all the fullness of God. Now to Him who is able to do immeasurably more than all we ask or imagine, according to His power that is at work within us...*
>
> *Ephesians 3:17-20*

What does Paul pray will fill you? _____

Being filled with the fullness of God means I have to die to something in my life to make room for Him. I must die to anger if I am to be filled with love. I must die to my own desires if I am to be filled with His desires. I must die to the wrong attitudes if I am to be filled with the right attitudes. Being filled with the fullness of God means that you and I are willing to come under His control through the power of the Holy Spirit. The Holy Spirit is Jesus Himself. In other words, the indwelling Holy Spirit controls the Spirit-filled person, just as alcohol can control a person who is drunk. Neither person needs to proclaim what fills them, because it shows.

Have you ever been on a horse that has never been ridden? If you have, then you know he will try to buck you off. If you are a good equestrian, you will climb back on until the horse gives up having his own way. We are like that horse. Once we give up having our way, we give our attention to our Master. If He wants us to go forward, we do. If He wants us to stop, we do. If He wants us to turn around, we do. That's being filled with the Spirit. And when you and I are under His control, we will walk in a worthy manner.

Let's look at a few verses that reveal the One who is able to help us walk in a worthy manner.

Now to Him who is able to do exceeding abundantly beyond all that we

ask or think, according to the power that works within us.
Ephesians 3:20

What is God able to do for you today? _____

Now, Lord, consider their threats and enable your servants to speak your word with great boldness.
Acts 4:29 (NIV)

And God is able to make all grace abound to you, that always having all sufficiency in everything, you may have an abundance for every good deed.
2 Corinthians 9:8

For it is God who is at work in you, both to will and to work for His good pleasure.
Philippians 2:13

Do not lie to one another, since you laid aside the old self with its evil practices, and have put on the new self who is being renewed to a true knowledge according to the image of the One who created him.
Colossians 3:9-10

Journal

From any of today's reading what is it you would ask God to do for you concerning your walk with Him?

_____

_____

_____

_____

_____

_____

_____

_____

_____

_____

_____

_____

Day 63: 1 Corinthians 15:1-8,54-58

Now I make known to you, brethren, the gospel which I preached to you, which also you received, in which also you stand, by which also you are saved, if you hold fast the word which I preached to you, unless you believed in vain. For I delivered to you as of first importance what I also received, that Christ died for our sins according to the Scriptures, and that He was buried, and that He was raised on the third day according to the Scriptures, and that He appeared to Cephas, then to the twelve. After that He appeared to more than five hundred brethren at one time, most of whom remain until now, but some have fallen asleep; then He appeared to James, then to all the apostles; and last of all, as it were to one untimely born, He appeared to me also.

But when this perishable will have put on the imperishable, and this mortal will have put on immortality, then will come about the saying that is written, "DEATH IS SWALLOWED UP in victory. O DEATH, WHERE IS YOUR VICTORY? O DEATH, WHERE IS YOUR STING?" The sting of death is sin, and the power of sin is the law; but thanks be to God, who gives us the victory through our Lord Jesus Christ. Therefore, my beloved brethren, be steadfast, immovable, always abounding in the work of the Lord, knowing that your toil is not in vain in the Lord.

Some of the Corinthians were denying the resurrection of the dead. "Now if Christ is preached, that He has been raised from the dead, how do some among you say that there is no resurrection of the dead?" (1 Corinthians 15:12) Christ's death and resurrection is the foundation of Christianity. Remove this foundation and all our hopes for victory over sin and death will disappear. Remove His sacrifice and we cannot understand what a valuable, priceless possession we are.

In 1 Corinthians 15:2-4, Paul gives the plan of salvation. Today we call it the "Good News." It is good news because Christ's death and resurrection prove we are His most valuable possession. The best is yet to come for us! Shouldn't we live now to give Him our best?

Illustration

As a child, I was highly allergic to bee stings. That made the bees in our little playhouse even more frightening to me. I guess that's why this story has such an impact on my life.

One spring day, a little boy and his father were driving down a country road. Suddenly, a bumblebee flew in the car window. Since the little boy was deathly allergic to bee stings, he became petrified. The father, seeing his son's distress, quickly reached out, grabbed the bee, squeezed it in his hand, and then released it. As soon as he let go, the little boy became frantic when the bee buzzed by him once again. His father saw his panic-stricken face, reached out his hand and pointed to his palm. There, still stuck in the skin, was the bee's stinger. "Do you see that?" he said. "You don't need to be afraid anymore. I've taken the sting for you." [10]

We no longer need to be afraid of death, no matter how or when it comes to us. Christ faced death for us. He has taken the sting! He has risen! Fear is gone. Eternal life is ours.

Journal

What has the LORD highlighted to you through today's reading?

_____

_____

_____

_____

_____

_____

_____

_____

_____

_____

_____

_____

Application

Do you fear death? If you do, why? Do you understand that He has taken the sting for you? From the following verses, how valuable are you? "Knowing that you were not redeemed with perishable things like silver or gold from your futile way of life inherited from your forefathers, but with precious blood, as of a lamb unblemished and spotless, the blood of Christ." 1 Peter 1:18-19 What will you do today to give Him your best? He gave His best for you.

Principle

Christ's life, death and resurrection prove we are His most valuable possession.

Day 64: Apply this principle to your life
Christ's life, death and resurrection prove
we are His most valuable possession.

As a believer, all you have to do in order to know how valuable you are is to look closely at the cross. He gave up His life so you may live. He suffered death so you might escape it. For even though your mortal body will die, you will never be separated from the Father.

Jesus is a picture of the Suffering Servant. His life was a divine paradox.

Jesus was hungry (Matthew 4:2)...yet He fed multitudes. (John 6)
Jesus was thirsty (John 19:28)...yet He is the water of life. (John 4:14)
Jesus was weary (John 4:6)...yet He is our rest. (Matthew 11:29)
Jesus prayed (Mark 14:32)...yet He hears our prayers. (John 14:13-14)
Jesus wept (John 11:35)...yet He dries our tears. (Revelation 21:4)
Jesus was put to death (John 19:16)...yet He will raise us from the dead. (Eph. 2:6)

We, as believers, have a living hope through the resurrection of Jesus Christ.

> *Blessed be the God and Father of our Lord Jesus Christ, who according to His great mercy has caused us to be born again to a living hope through the resurrection of Jesus Christ from the dead.*   *1 Peter 1:3*

Jesus treasures you so much that He came to earth to die for you. He values you so much that He will raise you from the dead in order to live with you for all eternity.

When Jesus was praying to the Father in John 17:6, we can see that we are His most valuable possession:

> *I have revealed you to those whom you gave me out of the world. They were yours; you gave them to me and they have obeyed your word.*
> *John 17:6*

What is your most valuable possession? I'm not talking about family or loved ones. When I look down at my ring on my left hand, I am looking at my most valuable possession. Not because of the cost or what it looks like, even though it is beautiful. It is my most valuable possession because of the story behind it.

When my mother was pregnant with me, her sister was dying with cancer. Their last time together, my mom shared with her that she was going to name her child after her. I'm that child and that's why my name is Frances. When my Aunt Frances heard that, she took off her ring and gave it to my mom and asked her to give it to me after I was old enough to wear it. It was her birthstone because she was born in January. Guess when I was born? You got it. January.

I can remember getting this ring out of my mom's jewelry box and trying it on for years. One day I decided to put the ring on and go play outside. I lost it. I don't even remember getting in trouble. I guess my mom saw I was upset enough. As an adult, whenever I would pass a jewelry store, I would always look to see if there was a ring like the one Aunt Frances had given me. I NEVER found one. Then, without ever having told that story to my husband, I opened my Christmas present from him a few years ago and it was a ring identical to Aunt Frances' ring! I believe the LORD allowed me to receive this ring again to re-mind me how valuable I am to Him. What a wonderful reminder I carry with me every day as I look at this ring. Jesus left us a great gift and reminder of His love: the Cross.

> *Are not two sparrows sold for a cent? And yet not one of them will fall to the ground apart from your Father. But the very hairs of your head are all numbered. Therefore do not fear; you are of more value than many sparrows.* *Matthew 10:29-31*

> *When I consider Thy heavens, the work of Thy fingers, the moon and the stars, which Thou hast ordained; what is man, that Thou dost take thought of him? And the son of man, that Thou dost care for him? Yet Thou hast made him a little lower than God, and dost crown him with glory and majesty!* *Psalm 8:3-5*

Journal

What reminds you that you are valuable to Him?

_____

_____

_____

_____

_____

_____

_____

_____

_____

_____

_____

_____

Day 65: Psalm 77:1-12,18-20

For the choir director; according to Jeduthun. A Psalm of Asaph.

My voice rises to God, and I will cry aloud; My voice rises to God, and He will hear me. In the day of my trouble I sought the Lord; In the night my hand was stretched out without weariness; My soul refused to be comforted. When I remember God, then I am disturbed; When I sigh, then my spirit grows faint.

Selah.

Thou hast held my eyelids open; I am so troubled that I cannot speak. I have considered the days of old, The years of long ago. **I will remember my song in the night; I will meditate with my heart; And my spirit ponders.** *Will the Lord reject forever? And will He never be favorable again? Has His loving-kindness ceased forever? Has His*

promise come to an end forever? Has God forgotten to be gracious? Or has He in anger withdrawn His compassion?

Selah.

Then I said, "It is my grief, That the right hand of the Most High has changed." I shall remember the deeds of the LORD; Surely I will remember Thy wonders of old. I will meditate on all Thy work, And muse on Thy deeds.

The sound of Thy thunder was in the whirlwind; The lightnings lit up the world; The earth trembled and shook. Thy way was in the sea, And Thy paths in the mighty waters, And Thy footprints may not be known. Thou didst lead Thy people like a flock, By the hand of Moses and Aaron.

The psalmist Asaph cried out from an anxious heart in the night to God. Asaph felt abandoned and insecure. He felt the Lord was withholding His compassion, love and favor. Asaph's problem was that he was going by what he "felt," not by trusting the One he knew. Somehow Asaph needed to return to living in the will rather than in emotions. God does His greatest work through our wills, not in our emotions. Finally in verse 11, Asaph finds comfort and courage from God, Who is: **holy, strong, mighty, great, powerful and sovereign**.

Illustration

I'm usually in bed by this time of night…but since I can't sleep, I have decided to go into my office to meditate on God's Word. My heart is heavy with the burdens of several people I love. I am struggling because I cannot see evidence that God is working in my friends' lives. After reading Psalm 77, I felt like Asaph, because I too am struggling between what I feel and the One I know. The problem is there are two different people sitting in my chair tonight: Emmy and Willy.

Emotional Emmy says: "I don't *feel* like God is working, so I'm down."

Trusting Will says: "I may not be able to *see* what God is doing right now, but I know He is working."

Emotional Emmy says: "I don't *feel* like praying tonight, so I won't."

Trusting Will says: "I don't *feel* like praying tonight, but I will."

Emotional Emmy says: "I don't *feel* like going to Bible study, so I'll stay home and watch television."

Trusting Will says: "I don't *feel* like going to Bible Study, but I know that is where I need to be."

Jesus probably didn't feel like dying on the cross – but by an act of His will, He died for us.

Now that I'm acting out of my will instead of my emotions, I think I can sleep. It's amazing how fast we can move from doubting to resting when we live in our will, submitted to His will, rather than in our feelings. For I have great confidence in my God, Who never slumbers nor sleeps, but Who is always working out His purpose for our lives.

Application

Do you have the same struggle between living in your will or in your emotions? Are you mostly Emmy or Willy today? Could it be that you are living in fear and doubt because you are acting out of your emotions rather than your will? If you don't feel like going to Bible study this week, what will you do?

Journal

What has the LORD highlighted to you through today's reading?

_____

_____

_____

_____

_____

_____

_____

_____

Principle

God does His greatest work in your will, not your emotions.

Day 66: Apply this principle to your life

God does His greatest work in your will, not your emotions.

Writing about what God says is much easier than living it out. I was asked many years ago to be a leader in a Bible study. I prayed and believed that God wanted me to be one, but I responded with a "no" because I didn't feel like being a leader that year. So, I was put in someone else's group and was miserable because I knew in my heart that God had called me to be a leader. I confessed to the Lord and pleaded with Him to give me another chance. He did. But it was two years later.

What is it you aren't doing because you don't feel like doing it? _____

_____

_____

It's time for us to stop and listen to the promises and commands of God. Since God is never wrong, we can trust what He says. We need to remember that in God's kingdom, faith is based on promises, not feelings.

Are you basing your faith on His promises and commands or your feelings?

_____

In Acts 27, Paul was on a ship that was about to sink because of a violent storm. After many days of being tossed about, Paul stood up and gave a promise from the LORD – they would all live. As the ship rocked back and forth from the storm, I wonder what the people on the ship thought about Paul? But Paul continued encouraging them because he knew that God is never wrong.

There will come a time in all our lives when we will be on a sinking ship and will need to hear and believe whatever God says. Let's look at some of the promises and commands of God and see how we can begin today believing them with our entire mind and heart simply because it's His Word.

God's promises and commands are trustworthy:

> *Consider it all joy, my brethren, when you encounter various trials.*
>
> *James 1:2*

What trial are you going through now that you consider a joy? _____

_____

_____

_____

James knew we live out of our wills and emotions. This command is one that doesn't come naturally to us. But knowing we can consider our trials joy because He will help us and grow us up in the process, we can do it by an act of our will.

And being fully assured that what He had promised, He was able also to perform.   *Romans 4:21*

For His anger is but for a moment, His favor is for a lifetime; weeping may last for the night, but a shout of joy comes in the morning.
Psalm 30:5

When you pass through the waters, I will be with you; and through the rivers, they will not overflow you. When you walk through the fire, you will not be scorched, nor will the flame burn you.   *Isaiah 43:2*

And the Lord said, "If you had faith like a mustard seed, you would say to this mulberry tree, 'Be uprooted and be planted in the sea'; and it would obey you."   *Luke 17:6*

Truly, truly, I say to you, he who believes in Me, the works that I do shall he do also; and greater works than these shall he do; because I go to the Father.   *John 14:12*

And you will seek Me and find Me, when you search for Me with all your heart.   *Jeremiah 29:13*

Therefore, my beloved brethren, be steadfast, immovable, always abounding in the work of the Lord, knowing that your toil is not in vain in the Lord.   *1 Corinthians 15:58*

Now he who plants and he who waters are one; but each will receive his own reward according to his own labor.   *1 Corinthians 3:8*

Journal

What one promise of God from today's reading stood out to you?

_____

_____

_____

_____

_____

_____

_____

Day 67: 1 Peter 1:1-9

Peter, an apostle of Jesus Christ, to those who reside as aliens, scattered throughout Pontus, Galatia, Cappadocia, Asia, and Bithynia, who are chosen according to the foreknowledge of God the Father, by the sanctifying work of the Spirit, that you may obey Jesus Christ and be sprinkled with His blood: May grace and peace be yours in fullest measure.

Blessed be the God and Father of our Lord Jesus Christ, who according to His great mercy has caused us to be born again to a living hope through the resurrection of Jesus Christ from the dead, to obtain an inheritance which is imperishable and undefiled and will not fade away, reserved in heaven for you,

who are protected by the power of God through faith for a salvation ready to be revealed in the last time. In this you greatly rejoice, even though now for a little while, if necessary, you have been distressed by various trials, that the proof of your faith, being more precious than gold which is perishable, even though tested by fire, may be found to result in praise and glory and honor at the revelation of Jesus Christ; **and though you have not seen Him, you love Him, and though you do not see Him now, but believe in Him, you greatly rejoice with joy inexpressible and full of glory, obtaining as the outcome of your faith the salvation of your souls.**

Peter was known as the Apostle of Hope. The early Christians, like us, were in need of hope. So Peter wrote to them describing his own personal experience of being with Jesus. Peter had been an eyewitness to His life, death and ascension to heaven. Even though these Christians believed in Jesus, they had never seen Him. Peter shares in verse 9 that the final goal of their faith would be to see Jesus and live with Him forever. Peter wanted to share the hope he had in the living, loving, reigning, returning Savior, Who has given all Christians an inheritance no one can take away. This inheritance begins the moment one accepts Him as Lord and Savior.

Illustration

From the age of 10, William Dyke was blind. As a young man, he fell in love. Even though he had never seen her, they set a wedding date. During their engagement, a new surgical procedure for blindness was announced. They decided to operate on William. Although they believed the surgery was a success, they planned that the bandages would not be removed until the wedding.

As the music began, the pastor came forward with William. He stood, both eyes wrapped in gauze, waiting for his bride. When the last bridesmaid found her place, William's physician snipped the bandages, unwrapped the gauze and removed the pads.

This man, who had been blind since he was 10 years old, SAW for the first time, the face of the one whom he had not seen, but loved.

It will be that way when we see Jesus. The only difference is we will be the blind ones, and He will remove the bandages that bind our eyes, so we can see our living, loving, reigning Lord Jesus for the first time. [11]

Journal

What has the LORD highlighted to you through today's reading?

_____

_____

_____

_____

_____

_____

_____

_____

_____

_____

_____

_____

_____

_____

_____

_____

Application

Even though you have never seen Jesus, do you love Him? Do you love Him and believe in Him so much that your joy is sometimes inexpressible? Are you looking forward to seeing Him face to face or does that truth frighten you? Will you read verses 8 and 9 again and ask Him to make those words a reality in your life?

Principle

Hope is found in our living, loving, reigning, and returning Savior, Jesus.

Day 68: *Apply this principle to your life*

Hope is found in our living, loving, reigning, and returning Savior, Jesus.

Peter was now part of the evidence that Jesus was alive. So am I. So are you. People are watching us to see what Jesus really can do in a person's life. A friend shared a very convicting story with me.

A father called his son who was off at college. He had a question he wanted to ask him in person. They set up a time to meet the next day for lunch at a restaurant off-campus. After hearing about his son's week, the father asked him, "Son, what is it in my life that keeps you from being all you can be for Christ?" I can almost hear Peter say those very words to us today.

We may all have different vocations in life, but we have all been given the same mission. The final instruction that King Jesus gave in Matthew 28 is called "The Great Commission." It applies to all believers. Our mission is to go share Jesus with the world. The world that needs hope. The world that needs to know our living, loving, reigning, and (one day) returning, Savior. We are called to bring His light into a dark world. When we realize that this is our mission in life, then our lives will take on new meaning.

> *And Jesus came up and spoke to them, saying, "All authority has been given to Me in heaven and on earth. Go therefore and make disciples of all the nations, baptizing them in the name of the Father and the Son and the Holy Spirit, teaching them to observe all that I commanded you; and lo, I am with you always, even to the end of the age."   Matthew 28:18-20*

How do you see your mission in life?_____

_____

_____

_____

_____

Here are a couple of verses that I have been praying for my family and me. My prayer is that the salvation of others be the joy and passion of our lives.

> *Brethren, my heart's desire and my prayer to God for them is for their salvation.   Romans 10:1*

> *For what is it we live for, that gives us hope and joy and is our proud reward and crown? It is you! Yes, you will bring us much joy as we stand*

together before our Lord Jesus Christ when he comes back again. For
you are our trophy and joy.　　　*1 Thessalonians 2:19-20 (TLB)*

WHEN CHRIST COMES BACK,
There will be no more chances to suffer for Him.
There will be no more chances to sacrifice for Him.
There will be no more chances to speak for Him.
There will be no more chances to live by faith.
There will be no more chances to prove our loyalty to Him.

Journal

How would you respond if Jesus said the following to you: "You are not living the life I died to give you"?

_____

Day 69: 2 Peter 1:1-8,12-18

Simon Peter, a bond-servant and apostle of Jesus Christ, to those who have received a faith of the same kind as ours, by the righteousness of our God and Savior, Jesus Christ: Grace and peace be multiplied to you in the knowledge of God and of Jesus our Lord; seeing that His divine power has granted to us everything pertaining to life and godliness, through the true knowledge of Him who called us by His own glory and excellence. For by these He has granted to us His precious and magnificent promises, in order that by them you might become partakers of the divine nature, having escaped the corruption that is in the world by lust. Now for this very reason also, applying all diligence, in your faith supply moral excellence, and in your moral excellence, knowledge; and in your knowledge, self-control, and in your self-control, perseverance, and in your perseverance, godliness; and in your godliness, brotherly kindness, and in your brotherly kindness, love. For if these qualities are yours and are increasing, they render you neither useless nor unfruitful in the true knowledge of our Lord Jesus Christ.

Therefore, I shall always be ready to remind you of these things, even though you already know them, and have been established in the truth which is present with you. And I consider it right, as long as I am in this earthly dwelling, to stir you up by way of reminder, *knowing that the laying aside of my earthly dwelling is imminent, as also our Lord Jesus Christ has made clear to me. And I will also be diligent that at any time after my departure you may be able to call these things to mind. For we did not follow cleverly devised tales when we made known to you the power and coming of our Lord Jesus Christ, but we were eyewitnesses of His majesty. For when He received honor and glory from God the Father, such an utterance as this was made to Him by the Majestic Glory, "This is My beloved Son with whom I am well-pleased"— and we ourselves heard this utterance made from heaven when we were with Him on the holy mountain.*

Peter was aware that his own death was near. He even describes his death as a 'departure' in verse 15. Peter saw death as a journey from this life to eternal life. He describes this new, lasting life in verses 16-18, when he witnessed it on the Mount of Transfiguration. He looked forward to experiencing it again for himself, for all eternity. Until then, he continued to write so that when his departure time came, the Christians would be able to recall the truth of God's Word. Peter knew that even Christians need to be reminded often of the Truth.

Illustration

I received a phone call and learned that one of my high school friends was rapidly losing her four year battle with cancer. I called her husband to ask if I could visit her. He suggested I come the next day. He also said that I should be prepared to do most of the talking, since the tumor was now wrapped around the part of her brain that controls speech and memory.

When I walked in, there she was, sitting up on the couch and speaking volumes of welcome with her eyes and smile. I hugged her and helped her lie down, because I knew that even sitting upright was a struggle for her. Knowing that she loved the Lord, I brought some unfinished pages of this book to share with her. I often stopped reading and asked her to sleep for awhile. She would sleep some and then wake up asking me to read to her some more. She would often interrupt me in the middle of a sentence, point her finger at me and struggle to speak: "Don't...give up. Finish." Knowing what a prayer warrior she was, I had previously asked her to pray for me to complete this book. Not only did she encourage me with her words, but with her life. She never gave up believing that the Lord loved her and was still in control of her life. She even communicated to me that day that she knew God would continue to answer her prayers, even if she never physically saw them answered.

As I drove home, I had a couple of hours to think about our day. I had read the Scripture above during one of her naps, and as I am using it now to share this experience, I desire more than ever to finish this book so that even after my departure, you may be able to call these things to mind and share them with someone else.

Journal

What has the LORD highlighted to you through today's reading?

_____

_____

_____

Application

What are some ways you are being reminded about the Truth? How are you being diligent to remind others about the Truth? What do you think will be the most meaningful thing you will leave behind for your loved ones? How often do you need to be reminded of God's power, love and truth?

Principle

Even Christians need to be reminded of God's Truths.

Day 70: Apply this principle to your life

Even Christians need to be reminded of God's Truths.

My dad is now in a nursing home several states away. He lives on the floor with other Alzheimer's patients. I love it when my brother and sister go with me to visit him. We usually have to remind him who we are. Sometimes he remembers us and sometimes he doesn't. It is so comforting to watch our Mom and the nurses taking such good care of him. They very kindly and patiently remind him when to get up, when it's time to eat, and when to go to bed.

It's always a bittersweet experience when we are there. Our last visit with him was very special. Somehow, I ended up in the room alone with him for a few minutes. So I went over and sat beside him on his bed and asked him if he wanted me to tell him some stories about Jesus. He nodded yes, so I did. Somehow it seems like he should be the one tucking me in bed, telling me stories, but I still loved reminding him about Jesus.

You and I may not have Alzheimer's, but we do forget about God much too often as we get too busy or too self-centered or too caught up in the things of the world. That's why God tells us over and over that we need to be reminded and to remind others of Who He is and how we are to live.

I used to put a note with Scripture on it in my children's lunch sacks. I believe the Lord gave me that idea one day when I was reading Deuteronomy 6:5-7:

And you shall love the LORD your God with all your heart and with all your soul and with all your might. And these words, which I am commanding you today, shall be on your heart; and you shall teach them diligently to your sons and shall talk of them when you sit in your house and when you walk by the way and when you lie down and when you rise up.

We are to remind others:

For this reason I have sent to you Timothy, who is my beloved and faithful child in the Lord, and he will remind you of my ways which are in Christ, just as I teach everywhere in every church.   *1 Corinthians 4:17*

In pointing out these things to the brethren, you will be a good servant of Christ Jesus, constantly nourished on the words of the faith and of the sound doctrine which you have been following.   *1 Timothy 4:6*

This is now, beloved, the second letter I am writing to you in which I am stirring up your sincere mind by way of reminder.   *2 Peter 3:1*

We are to be reminded:

Only give heed to yourself and keep your soul diligently, lest you forget the things which your eyes have seen, and lest they depart from your heart all the days of your life; but make them known to your sons and your grandsons.
Deuteronomy 4:9

And they forgot His deeds, and His miracles that He had shown them.
Psalm 78:11

For this reason we must pay much closer attention to what we have heard, lest we drift away from it.
Hebrews 2:1

Thus the sons of Israel did not remember the Lord their God, who had delivered them from the hands of all their enemies on every side.
Judges 8:34

We are to remember Him when we are away from home:

When I scatter them among the peoples, they will remember Me in far countries, and they with their children will live and come back.
Zechariah 10:9

We are to remember Him at night:

When I remember Thee on my bed, I meditate on Thee in the night watches.
Psalm 63:6

We are to remember Him in times of trouble:

While I was fainting away, I remembered the Lord; and my prayer came to Thee, into Thy holy temple.
Jonah 2:7

Journal

Thank God for all the times He has reminded you of Him, and then write one of the above Scriptures that you need to put into practice more often.

_____

_____

_____

_____

_____

_____

Epilogue

In Psalm 30:9 David wrote: "What profit is there in my blood, if I go down to the pit? Will the dust praise Thee? Will it declare Thy faithfulness?" When I read these words in 1996, I was challenged to look at what profit I will leave when I die. Will my dust praise the Lord? I realized the legacy I leave behind must be planned now. But what can I leave that has value? My high school track coach once said: "Three things are eternal: God, His Word, and people. Invest your life in these three." I have attempted to base my legacy on what is eternal.

In this book Fran Miller has put before you eternal truths which you can apply to your life. Her goal in writing this book was to make an investment, an eternal investment, in you. If you apply these truths and pass them on to others, you become her legacy. It is Fran's prayer that you choose the eternal.

May I encourage you today to continue your study of God's Word, thereby investing in the eternal. Will your dust praise the Lord?

S Faithe Finley
President, Master Design

Endnotes

1. Paul Lee Tan, ThD., *Encyclopedia of 7700 Illustrations* (Rockville, MD: Assurance Publishers, 1979), 1309.

2. Michael P. Green, ed., *Illustrations for Biblical Preaching* (Grand Rapids, MI: Baker Book House, 1985), 170.

3. Ibid., 220.

4. Matthew Henry, *The Matthew Henry Commentary* (Grand Rapids, MI: Zondervan, 1961), 304.

5. Charles R. Swindoll, *The Tale of the Tardy Oxcart* (Nashville, TN: Word Publishing, 1998), 509-510.

6. Green, 393.

7. Ibid., 325.

8. Ibid., 138.

9. Unknown, "The Dash".

10. Green, 96.

11. Green, 184.

Scripture Index

Gaze at God

Topical Index

If you would like to schedule Fran Miller
for your conference or retreat, please write:

Fran Miller
704 W. Clover Drive
Memphis, Tennessee 38120
email address: GazeatGod@aol.com